AF334204

J. O. McClurkan, 1861–1914

J. O. McClurkan:

His Life, His Theology, and Selections from His Writings

VOLUME TWO
TREVECCA CENTENNIAL SERIES

J. O. McClurkan: His Life, His Theology and Selections from His Writings
ISBN: 0-9657278-1-5

© 1998 by Trevecca Nazarene University
Published by Trevecca Press of Trevecca Nazarene University, 333 Murfreesboro Road, Nashville, TN 37210-2877

Printed in the United States of America.

Book design by Morley Concept+Design

Second Printing, 2001

J. O. McClurkan:

HIS LIFE, HIS THEOLOGY, AND SELECTIONS FROM HIS WRITINGS

William J. Strickland
with H. Ray Dunning

JANICE M. GREATHOUSE
GENERAL EDITOR,
TREVECCA CENTENNIAL SERIES

TREVECCA PRESS
NASHVILLE • TENNESSEE • 1998

Contents

Dedication

To my devoted wife, Martha, for her encouragement and patience during the course of this project, and to our son, Bill Jr., and our daughter and son-in-law, Susan and Kevin Poe,

To my former college professors who instilled in me a love of religious studies and history and whom I highly esteem, Dr. William M. Greathouse (religion) and Dr. Homer J. Adams (history),

And to my father, Rev. S. W. Strickland, who was a student of J. O. McClurkan from 1908 to 1914, teacher and academic administrator in Trevecca College for twelve years, Nazarene pastor and district superintendent, and author of *A New Look at Rev. J. O. McClurkan* (1960).

William J. Strickland

Acknowledgments

My sincere thanks go to Dr. H. Ray Dunning, my faculty colleague at Trevecca for thirty-one years and a recognized Wesleyan theologian, for writing the chapter on "J. O. McClurkan's Theology" and for assisting me with the chapter on "Selections from the Writings of J. O. McClurkan," as well as for proofreading the manuscript and offering valuable suggestions.

Others who have read the manuscript and given helpful feedback include Dr. Millard Reed, president of Trevecca Nazarene University; Dr. William Greathouse, Nazarene general superintendent emeritus, former president of Nazarene Theological Seminary and Trevecca Nazarene College, and my former college professor; Dr. Homer Adams, former president and dean of Trevecca Nazarene College and my former college professor; Dr. John Chilton, professor of history at Trevecca Nazarene University and member of the Trevecca Historical Committee; Dr. Gary Henecke, pastor of First Church of the Nazarene, Nashville, Tennessee; Jan Greathouse, director of public information at Trevecca Nazarene University and editor of the Trevecca Centennial Series; and Marian Jewell who assisted Jan Greathouse in the proofreading and editing process.

My appreciation is also extended to Chuck Haselwood, senior religion major at Trevecca Nazarene University, for typing the manuscript; and to Pam Crandall, Trevecca archivist, who assisted me in locating some of the helpful documents for this study.

William J. Strickland

Foreword

A POTENTIAL READER HAS THE RIGHT TO ASK, "WHY ANOTHER BOOK? Why this book in particular? Why revisit the work and writings of a man who has been dead since 1914?"

For those of us who are a part of the two organizations that came into being out of J. O. McClurkan's ministry (Nashville's First Church of the Nazarene and Trevecca Nazarene University), the answers to those questions are obvious. It is our centennial time, and we are eager to embrace the institutional memory. But is there a reason for you who do not share that particular relationship to learn about the founder of these institutions? I believe there is.

My belief arises out of the way in which history seems to reflect recurring patterns of challenges and responses. This repetition may be seen by recalling the last 200 years or so of the "holiness movement." In the eighteenth century, in a situation of spiritual decline, John Wesley gave leadership to a movement that some have considered the greatest spiritual movement of the last two hundred years. Wesley summoned believers to hear the call of God to salvation by grace through both faith and holy living. Unlike numerous unbalanced emphases throughout the history of Christian spirituality, Wesley kept these two in proper balance. Truth, he would maintain, finds expression in "both-and" rather than in "either-or" terms.

About a century later, during a period when holiness revivals were revitalizing the church in America, another holiness preacher expressed similar sentiments. J. O. McClurkan, like Wesley, saw truth as "both-and." He recognized the importance of the Calvinist emphasis on grace as well as the Arminian stress on human responsibility and intentionally attempted to integrate these two traditions in his preaching.

Also like Wesley, he grappled with the tension between structure and passion. He insisted on holding each in polar tension. Both men held the organized church in high esteem. Neither man left the church of his ordination although the followers of each eventually either formed or united with new denominations. Even though they had a high regard for the church, they both also realized that the passion of the movement must move beyond the organizational structure. Both seemed to have sensed intuitively that the spirit of holiness and the sectarian spirit are contradictory. Each held that perfect love in humility cannot arbitrarily exclude a brother or his sincere position if it is within the broader parameters of classical Christianity.

Now we are entering the third century of the Wesleyan movement. What may we expect during this period? Again the winds of the Spirit seem to be blowing among us. There is more discussion and interest in the subject of holiness now than at any time in the last half-century. But, unfortunately, this interest is also accompanied by widespread confusion to the degree that many have concluded that the holiness movement is in a debilitating identity crisis. Can we find wisdom from Wesley and McClurkan to give guidance to this new and challenging era? Do not their balanced emphases have relevance to counter potential imbalances in our theology? Does not their avoidance of the sectarian spirit warn us against a devastating divisiveness?

An hour of awesome opportunity lies before us. In the gracious will of the Father the Spirit of holiness may sweep across the world. All who pray for such a continued movement and work may learn from these who have preceded us by one and by two centuries.

Millard C. Reed

President, Trevecca Nazarene University

1998

Preface

Professors William J. Strickland and H. Ray Dunning combine their scholarly talents to paint a memorable picture of J. O. McClurkan, father of the holiness movement in the Southeast and founder of Trevecca Nazarene University.

The picture of McClurkan that emerges in these pages is that of "a man sent from God," as Merle Heath, his daughter, describes him in her biography by that title.

Born and nurtured as a Cumberland Presbyterian, McClurkan was sanctified wholly under the preaching of Methodist evangelist Beverly Carradine when he (McClurkan) was a California pastor. Soon thereafter McClurkan rose to become a leading light in the holiness movement. In McClurkan's teaching, as Strickland and Dunning explain, John Wesley's doctrine of holiness was balanced by a Calvinistic emphasis on divine grace. This teaching encouraged the entirely sanctified to acknowledge their remaining humanity and to undergo a "deeper death to self" in their disciplined quest for spiritual fullness. Strickland and Dunning point out that it was McClurkan's concern to balance salvation by grace (Calvinism) and holy living (Wesleyanism) that led him to adopt the name Trevecca for his college, from the Welsh "Trevecka," the name of the school founded for similar reasons by Lady Huntingdon in Wales in 1768.

This book notes that while Brother McClurkan was theologically sensitive he was primarily a preacher/teacher of the gospel who modeled Christian holiness in a life of service and who sacrificially invested himself in preparing and sending forth evangelists and missionaries into what he believed was "the eleventh hour" of the gospel dispensation. After his death in 1914 at the young age of fifty-two, McClurkan's work joined the Church of the Nazarene.

In this volume professors Strickland and Dunning make a significant contribution to holiness literature. Professor Strickland writes as a second-generation Treveccan. His father, S. W. Strickland, was one of McClurkan's early students who himself extensively researched the origins of Trevecca, both in Wales and in Nashville. Dr. Strickland's additional research provides a concise overview of McClurkan's life and the origins of the Church of the Nazarene in the South and Trevecca Nazarene University. Dr. Dunning's insightful analysis of McClurkan's theology reveals the genius of McClurkan and his contribution to the holiness movement. Additionally, Strickland and Dunning have collected key passages from McClurkan's writings, passages that reveal McClurkan's practical theology. This centennial volume has timely significance for many different kinds of readers.

William M. Greathouse
President, Trevecca Nazarene College—1963–1968
General Superintendent Emeritus, Church of the Nazarene

Introduction

THE RESEARCH FOR AND WRITING OF THIS BOOK HAVE BEEN LABORS of love. Studying the godly life and ministry of Rev. J. O. McClurkan has been a rich and challenging spiritual experience. Reading and trying to catch the spirit recorded in the "Minutes" of the Pentecostal Tabernacle, Mission, and college he founded, as well as reading McClurkan's own writings and the other excellent sources available, have inspired this writer. Here was a man who was characterized by his depth of spirituality, Christian tolerance, intense missionary fervor, and love and compassion for all sorts of people. He was a soul winner *par excellence.* His ministry was marked by a simplicity of goodness and greatness, combining excellent preaching and teaching skills, theoretical and practical education, grace and ethics. Theologically he attempted to build a bridge between the Arminian and Calvinistic systems of theology. This synthesis led him to a unique balance between the moment of "entire sanctification" and the human and more mature levels of Christian experience which recognized that after the moment there must be what he called a "deeper death to self."

Timothy L. Smith tells a story that illustrates the way in which McClurkan's views were in contrast to the popular theology of the American Holiness Movement. At a holiness conference in the South, McClurkan expressed his concern that, in preaching the eradication of the carnal mind in entire sanctification, holiness evangelists might fail to stress sufficiently the human frailties of those who enjoyed this sanctifying grace. Dr. H. C. Morrison interrupted and took McClurkan to task for some time. After Morrison finished his reproof, the saintly McClurkan, known for his gentleness, rose quietly, pointed to Morrison, and said, "Brethren, *that* is exactly what I mean."[1]

McClurkan was one who could not be hemmed in by denominationalism as a true Eleventh Hour laborer. His desire was not to oppose the churches, but to press on in holiness evangelism that affected all churches. He taught that "religion is love and… without love any and all religion is but a name."[2] His Tabernacle and Mission have borne much fruit as their influence lives on today through the First Church of the Nazarene in Nashville, the Tennessee and East Tennessee Districts of the Church of the Nazarene, and other areas and aspects of the Church of the Nazarene, including foreign missions and education. His Bible Training School was his family, and McClurkan's attitude toward the faculty and students was one of love and devotion in their mutual search for truth. That school continues today as the fully accredited Trevecca Nazarene University. His fervent prayer for his followers was that they would pursue holiness of heart and life. He was blessed with a high caliber of associates who gave excellent leadership in both ministerial and lay roles. S. W. Strickland, one of his former students, said, "Being under his preaching, educational, and pastoral ministry is that part of my heritage which I prize next to meeting my Lord and becoming a Christian."[3]

How does one explain the thought patterns and various theological and religious streams that influenced the life and ministry of J. O. McClurkan? In *The Trevecca Story*, Mildred Wynkoop identifies the following nine "streams" that converge in McClurkan's work: (1) *Cumberland Presbyterianism* gave him a flavor of Calvinism and a tremendous faith in God's sovereignty and keeping grace. (2) *Methodism* with its Arminianism and Wesleyan theology provided the background for holiness doctrine. (3) *The American Holiness Movement* led McClurkan to a personal experience of the grace of entire sanctification and emphasized an ecumenical and nonsectarian concept of holiness that made union with any denomination seem like a contradiction. (4) *Keswick Teachings* gave McClurkan an understanding of the humanness and fallibility of man even in the Spirit-filled Christian and the dynamic of the sanctified relationship. Thus he could speak about ever-increasing "deeper deaths to self" as well as "eradication" of inward sin.

(5) *The Christian and Missionary Alliance* contributed Keswick doctrine, missionary outreach, belief in the premillennial return of Christ, divine healing, the Eleventh Hour concept, and its preference to be considered a movement rather than a denomination. (6) *The Eleventh Hour Movement* emphasized the immediate premillennial return of Christ and gave a sense of urgency to evangelism, missions, and education, and shortcut methods to preparing for the work. (7) *Dispensationalism,* a type of interpretation of the Scripture associated with the nineteenth-century Prophetic Bible Conference Movement and popularized through the Scofield Bible, taught that history is divided into seven periods or dispensations in which God acts in different ways at different times, and it emphasized the premillennial return of Christ and a secret rapture of the Church. (8) *Wesleyan Fundamentalism* emphasized education in terms of Bible schools and institutes established primarily to indoctrinate and to be shortcuts to the preaching ministry. (9) *Mainline Nazarenism* represented by P. F. Bresee and H. Orton Wiley emphasized the importance of a liberal arts education as part of the total church concept. Of these influences, Wynkoop asserts, "All of these streams flowed into the McClurkan work and left powerful, sometimes indelible marks."[4] The most formative influence on McClurkan, she believes, was the American Holiness Movement, although Keswick teaching, Christian and Missionary Alliance doctrine, Cumberland Presbyterianism, and the Eleventh Hour Movement were significant influences also.[5]

It is virtually impossible to separate McClurkan, the man, from the Pentecostal Mission he founded, since the work was the shadow cast by this man. The Mission had eight main characteristics: (1) It was *nondenominational,* based on McClurkan's aversion for ecclesiasticism, on the influence of the Eleventh Hour Movement which said there is no time for denomination-building in light of the soon coming of Christ, and on the ecumenical and nonsectarian emphasis of the holiness movement. (2) *Preaching scriptural holiness* was a consuming passion. Scriptural holiness was understood as both crisis and process, involving a "deeper death to self" and seeking to combine the best in the Calvinist and Arminian systems of theology. (3) Its worship involved *"freedom in the Spirit"* that was genuine and wholesome, based on the dynamic presence of God. (4) It used *gospel music* that was uplifting and anointed by the Spirit of God. (5) It was committed to a *foreign missions program* in fulfillment of the Great Commission. (6) It possessed a *spirit of love and compassion for the needy* as expressed in social ministries, such as the Door of Hope, Training Home for Girls, and Trevecca Hospital. (7) It was concerned with spreading the message through *religious literature,* such as *Zion's Outlook/Living Water* (the main journal of communication among the followers of McClurkan), the writings of McClurkan, and other recommended holiness literature. (8) It stressed *education* as reflected in the Bible Training School and Trevecca College. All of these characteristics have a direct bearing on the life and ministry of J. O. McClurkan.

A few comments about the sources used for this study are in order. The primary sources include the various recorded "Minutes" of the Pentecostal Alliance (Mission). The sources of the "Minutes" were not always easy to sort out between the Pentecostal Tabernacle (local congregation church board), Pentecostal Alliance (Mission), annual conventions, and committees, such as General Committee, Executive Committee, Home Mission Committee (also a Home Mission Executive Committee), Foreign Mission Committee (also a Foreign Mission Executive Committee), and Camp Meeting Committee. Other primary sources were the issues of *Zion's Outlook* and *Living Water* plus the writings of McClurkan which include *Wholly Sanctified, How to Keep Sanctified, Behold He Cometh, Personal Work, Chosen Vessels,* and *The Ministry of Prayer.* McClurkan's correspondence with Nazarene leaders P. F. Bresee and H. F. Reynolds rounds out the primary sources.

Helpful secondary sources include the following: John T. Benson Jr., *History of the Pentecostal Mission, 1898–1915* (1977); Mildred Bangs Wynkoop, *The Trevecca Story* (1976); Jasper White's master's degree thesis at Indiana Central College, "A Man and a Mission: The Story of J. O. McClurkan and the Pentecostal Mission, 1898–1915" (1973); M. E. Redford's bachelor of divinity thesis at Vanderbilt University, "History of the Church of the Nazarene in Tennessee" (1934); Eugene Williams's bachelor of divinity thesis at Nazarene Theological Seminary, "History of Trevecca Nazarene College" (1956); Merle McClurkan Heath's intimate portrait of her father, *A Man Sent of God: The Life of J. O. McClurkan* (1947); S. W. Strickland, *A New Look at Rev. J. O. McClurkan* (1960); Timothy L. Smith, *Called Unto Holiness*

(1962), Chapter VIII—"The Pentecostal Mission in Tennessee, 1898–1915"; Millard Reed's paper submitted to Professor Eugene Te Selle at Vanderbilt University, "A Brief Study of the Pentecostal Mission" (1976); Founder's Day addresses at Trevecca by Emmett McClurkan (1945), C. E. Hardy (1946), and William M. Greathouse (1986); and the 1928 *Darda* which has a "Historical Sketch," which I assume was written by the editor, Claude Galloway.

In an effort to maintain the integrity of these sources, all quoted passages and the selections from McClurkan's writings (Chapter III) have been reproduced as they are in the originals. Variations in capitalization, punctuation, and usage will appear.

My desire for readers of this book has already been expressed by Dr. J. B. Chapman in his Foreword to Merle McClurkan Heath's *A Man Sent of God*. Chapman says, "The book will not make you want to be 'another McClurkan'…. But it will make you want to be your own best self. And it will make you want to spend and be spent for others." May it be so, as the mission lives on today.

William J. Strickland
Professor of Religion
Trevecca Nazarene University

---

¹ Timothy L. Smith, *Called Unto Holiness* (Kansas City: Nazarene Publishing House, 1962), 192.
²Ibid., 183.
³S. W. Strickland, *A New Look at J. O. McClurkan* (Nashville: Parthenon Press, 1960), 87.
⁴Mildred Bangs Wynkoop, *The Trevecca Story* (Nashville: Trevecca Press, 1976), 37.
⁵Ibid., 27–38.

CHAPTER ONE

Life of J. O. McClurkan

J. O. MCCLURKAN, A CUMBERLAND PRESBYTERIAN EVANGELIST, IS considered the father of the Wesleyan Holiness Movement in Middle Tennessee, the catalyst to organize the holiness people in the Southeast, and the founder of the school that became Trevecca Nazarene University.[1] While holiness work had begun in Tennessee about 1894, there was no strong leadership and, therefore, no great gains were made until the Pentecostal Alliance (later named Pentecostal Mission) developed in 1897-98 in Nashville, Tennessee, under the leadership of J. O. McClurkan. This book is the story of a man who was passionate about his service for Christ; his work resulted in the formation of one of the major groups that became a part of the Church of the Nazarene.

Early Life and Ministry

JAMES OCTAVIAS MCCLURKAN WAS BORN ON NOVEMBER 13, 1861, IN the Yellow Creek Community of Houston County, Tennessee, about sixty miles northwest of Nashville, between the small towns of Dickson and Erin. His grandfather, Hugh McClurkan, had come to America from Scotland and settled in Pittsburgh, Pennsylvania. His son, John McClurkan, J. O.'s father, left Pennsylvania and settled in the rural community of Yellow Creek in Houston County, Tennessee, where he became a schoolteacher and an itinerant preacher in the pioneer days of the Cumberland Presbyterian Church in Tennessee. McClurkan's mother was described in *Zion's Outlook* as "one of God's saints, brilliant, devoted to God's work, and to her family."[2] Dr. Mildred Wynkoop, in *The Trevecca Story*, describes the influence of this preacher's home on young McClurkan: "The depth of spiritual vitality and the congenial, friendly home atmosphere in the humble country farmhouse, left few if any scars on the children from the difficult war [Civil War] years. Ministers from all denominations gathered around the hospitable board in the log kitchen standing somewhat apart from the main house. 'J. O.'… remembered the earnest conversations and prayers heard in that room. They profoundly molded his young mind and created life goals never to be forgotten."[3]

The McClurkan family home

Brother McClurkan was one of thirteen children, the second of four preacher sons. Not only were prayer and regular church attendance vital parts of the family's life, but access to his father's library gave J. O. an early educational opportunity. He would read by candlelight or by the glowing embers from the fire, while lying on the hearth, until late in the night.[4] He was especially fond of the Bible, and when at five years of age he was offered a dollar by his mother if he would read the Bible through, he replied, "I am going to read it through anyway."[5] His daughter, Merle McClurkan Heath, analyzes the significance of J. O.'s father's library:

> It was this library of Grandfather's which laid for Father a foundation of an education beyond the limitations of the log schoolhouse, and implanted within him the rudiments of a theology which, if too sternly Calvinistic, he tempered in later years with the whosoever willness of the Arminian doctrine. He said that between the two dominant theories there is a meeting place. And he lived and taught at that level.
>
> The basic tenet of Calvinism… was imbedded in him like granite. The sovereignty of God! This conflicted in no way in his thinking with the free moral agency of man. Like Isaiah he saw God high and lifted up before whom he walked most humbly, and with whom he communed reverently. Indeed communion with God became the habit of his life. Prayer flowed through him like breath. Yet he took no liberties with God in language. His speech when talking with his Father was language becoming a child of the King.[6]

Conversion

J. O. McClurkan was converted at the age of thirteen on the last night of the fall revival at the old Bethany Cumberland Presbyterian Church in Yellow Creek. He had attended the revival every night with his mother and had been a constant seeker. After the last service of the meeting had been dismissed and others were headed home, J. O. remained in prayer along with his pastor and Sunday school teacher who were encouraging and instructing him. Little did they realize that "a great soul winner was then being born into the family of God, one whose pen and influence were to reach across the seas."[7]

Heath describes her father's salvation experience: "His conversion came as quietly as the breaking of the day with all the beauty and freshness and wonder of the dawn. When he walked out of that almost deserted church, he said that he walked into a new world, a world bathed in the glory of God. 'The stars,' he said, 'shone with a new luster. I had never seen the moon so brilliant. The atmosphere seemed charged with a fragrant aroma. The darkness was light. Behold, all things had become new.'"[8]

Call to Preach

Even before his life-changing spiritual conversion, J. O. McClurkan had felt that God was calling him to the ministry. This spiritual experience confirmed his call to preach. Heath recounts that "he described his call to the ministry as an inner urge, a conviction—the voice of God in his heart which never left him."[9]

J. O. and his father were very close friends and congenial spirits, spending much time together sharing aspirations, concerns, and dreams. They became a familiar sight—father and son mounted on horses leaving Saturday to make the father's Sunday appointments. One day while the horses were resting under the shade of the sycamore trees, J. O.'s father said to him, "Jim, I will preach at the morning service. You will preach at night."[10] And so, at the youthful age of seventeen, J. O. McClurkan began his active ministry. He learned to preach by preaching, just as he learned to pray and win souls by praying and winning souls. He made blunders but he was willing to try again. Here he found a method of education—to learn by doing—which along with formal educational studies helped to shape the lives of many men and women into vessels of honor and service.

In 1879 at age eighteen, J. O. was licensed to preach by the Charlotte Presbytery of the Tennessee Cumberland Presbyterian Church.[11] For the next few months he preached and taught school in the Yellow Creek Community.

Education and Marriage

McClurkan's exposure to the wide world of learning through his father's library doubtless generated in his young mind a yearning to go to college to better prepare himself for the ministry. At age nineteen, he entered Cloverdale College in Cloverdale, Tennessee, where he remained for only one year. Apparently he was unhappy with the emphasis on social status and disagreed with some of the beliefs of the headmaster, so the next year at the age of twenty he transferred to Trinity College, a Presbyterian school in Tehuacana, Texas, for his theological training.[12]

Already frail in body, McClurkan was stricken by a serious illness before the end of his first year at Trinity College. This condition, with which he wrestled the rest of his life, gave him a sympathetic understanding for all who suffered.

Trinity College, Tehuacana, Texas

Returning home for rest and recuperation, he married his childhood sweetheart, Martha Frances Rye, on November 15, 1882. Thomas Rye, her father, sternly predicted that Jim McClurkan would not live a year and that she would be "bringing home a young'un for me and your ma to raise." Her determined response was, "I'll show him ….If anything happens to Jimmie, I'll paddle my own canoe."[13] Into this union came one son and three daughters. Frances proved to be a stabilizing and supportive influence in J. O.'s life. She was described as "a young woman of commanding appearance; of full sweet voice; one of the best open-air speakers in our work."[14] Wynkoop describes Frances's partnership with J. O.: "She became an able preacher encouraged in her ministry by her husband, even preaching along with him in revival work. J. O. opposed the ordination of women, listing this [opposition] as one of his objections to uniting with the Church of the Nazarene, but approved women as preachers. Interestingly, Mrs. McClurkan was ordained a few years after the death of her husband, when the Pentecostal Mission joined forces with the Nazarene Church. She lived to be over one hundred years old."[15]

The next few years were difficult years for the newly married couple. McClurkan re-entered Trinity College in Texas, but because of his recurring illness he entered into a diversification of activities including teaching school, evangelizing, working on a newspaper, and, when he could, taking courses at Trinity. These were also difficult years financially for the young couple.[16]

J. O. McClurkan and his wife, Martha Frances

Pastorates

In 1886 at age twenty-five, McClurkan accepted his first pastorate as minister of the Cumberland Presbyterian Church in Decatur, Texas, where he served for two years. In this pastorate he infused new life into a congregation that was almost dead spiritually, and his leadership ability and preaching gifts were discovered by the presbytery.[17] Here he came to the awareness of a truth that was to undergird him in many difficult undertakings: "Every call of God carries with it the divine enablings," he said.[18]

At the age of twenty-seven, McClurkan felt led of the Lord to move westward to California in 1888, serving Cumberland Presbyterian pastorates at Visalia and Selma. Because of his experience and skill at revitalizing the lifeless churches to which he was sent, he was appointed synodical evangelist. McClurkan's daughter quotes her mother in describing these early pastorates in Texas and California as "like continuing revivals…. The altar was thrown open at the regular services, and people were converted and grew up into the sturdy new growth of the church."[19]

McClurkan's next pastorate in San Jose, California, was the most pivotal one in his Cumberland Presbyterian career and became the threshold to a new world. He was asked by his synod to go to San Jose to resurrect "a deserted, locked-up church."[20] Through house-to-house ministry, personal evangelism, a strong emphasis on prayer, and a dynamic youth ministry, within three years he had built up the church until it became the denomination's strongest church on the West Coast. About three hundred members were added to the church during his pastorate.

Dr. Beverly Carradine, Methodist holiness evangelist, under whose ministry J. O. McClurkan was sanctified.

A major turning point occurred in the McClurkans' life during this period. In 1895 the McClurkans were invited to attend a revival at the Methodist Church. Dr. Beverly Carradine, a leading Methodist holiness evangelist, was preaching about an experience which he called sanctification. McClurkan had never before heard holiness preaching with an emphasis on a "second blessing" called entire sanctification. In spite of being the highly respected Cumberland Presbyterian pastor of one of the largest churches in San Jose, McClurkan attended the meeting and sought for and quietly received the blessing of entire sanctification, an experience bringing a clean heart and the indwelling of the Holy Spirit.[21] Mrs. McClurkan came into the experience of holiness a few days later. S. W. Strickland, one of McClurkan's early students, says, "Receiving the experience of Entire Sanctification was the turning point in Bro. McClurkan's great career. He was a chosen vessel and destined to be one of the great holiness leaders of modern times."[22]

McClurkan immediately began to preach holiness doctrine in his own church, and many of his people received the same sanctifying grace. His preaching took on a new zeal and force.[23]

Even before the Carradine meeting, the McClurkans had been planning to visit their relatives in Tennessee. The San Jose church gave him a leave of absence for a year with a mutual expectation that he would return. However, their beloved pastor's life and work began to follow a different direction that never led back to San Jose and his waiting congregation.

When it became known that McClurkan was making the trip back to Tennessee, calls began coming for him to stop here and there across the country to hold revival meetings. His trip home was thus transformed under the hand of God into an evangelistic tour which continued for a two-year period. His wife and four children traveled with him.

When the McClurkan family finally arrived in Tennessee in the early months of 1897, J. O. was soon invited to preach in a revival in progress in his home community. Merle McClurkan Heath describes the Yellow Creek revival:

> When eventually he [McClurkan] did arrive, he found a revival meeting in progress in the old Trinity Church, which was conducted by his boyhood friend, Jim Rye. Of course, Father was invited to preach but he held back, not that he wanted to be urged, but that he might make it plain to Jim Rye just what he was preaching.
>
> "I am preaching a doctrine that is not popular in many churches and it might hurt you with your membership. I want you to think about it."
>
> "Are you preaching the Bible?" Brother Rye asked.
>
> "Yes, I am preaching the Bible as I understand it."
>
> "Well, then, go right ahead. I am not afraid of the Bible."

Thus it was Father preached his first sermon on "The Fullness of the Blessing" to his home community with the result that Brother Rye was himself gloriously sanctified in his own meeting and became not only the first fruits of Father's labor in Middle Tennessee but a mighty witness to the truth of holiness.[24]

The Pentecostal Alliance/Mission

WHILE MCCLURKAN WAS COMPLETING AN EVANGELISTIC TOUR THAT brought him to Middle Tennessee in 1897, his only son, Emmett, became critically ill and the parents were advised to take him to Nashville for medical treatment. Little did J. O. realize that providentially he and Nashville would have a work to do over the next seventeen years.

McClurkan's introduction to Nashville took place during Tennessee's great centennial celebration. There was much excitement with thousands of visitors coming and going. "It is reasonable to suppose that many people heard the gentle yet compelling voice of the 'Man Sent of God,'" says Wynkoop.[25] In addition, there were calls for revivals in the Nashville area from pastors (mostly Methodist) sympathetic to the message he was preaching. Holiness revivals were thus held in Methodist churches as well as under tents in various sections of the city. Within a few months McClurkan was surrounded by a group of men and women who were firm believers in holiness and wanted to share their newfound faith with others, as well as receive spiritual nourishment for their own hearts.[26] It should be noted that McClurkan was not introducing a new doctrine to Middle Tennessee in 1897, nor was he the first Wesleyan holiness preacher in the area.[27] Methodist pastor B. F. Haynes, who edited *Zion's Outlook* prior to McClurkan's group's taking it over in 1900, provides the following account of the origins of the holiness movement in Middle Tennessee: "Four years ago [1894] the Holiness Movement entered Middle Tennessee. Prior to this only a few rural districts had been reached by it while centers of population knew but little of this blessed truth. Within a short time a glorious revival wave swept over a large section of the state, embracing such points as Erin, Charlotte, Dickson, Clarksville, Franklin, and Nashville. Hundreds took the Lord Jesus for their sanctifier and many sinners accepted Him as their Savior."[28]

With the coming of winter in 1897 and the close of the summer tent campaign, Brother McClurkan was faced with the need to decide between his return to California and his obligation to the growing following of holiness people in and around Nashville who were looking to him for leadership.

The immediate answer came in an unexpected way, described by Heath as "a chain-lightning streak of trouble."[29] While on his way by train to an out-of-town appointment, McClurkan reached for his wallet and discovered that a pickpocket had relieved him of all his money. He hurried home to tell his story to Mrs. McClurkan who was not concerned about the money but about the red spots she saw on his face, spots which told her that he was sick. The illness turned out to be double pneumonia, a disease that was fatal in many cases. McClurkan was now fighting for his life and the end seemed to be near. While the doctors and nurses tried to prepare Mrs. McClurkan for her husband's death, her faith and confidence were in God. "He will get well," she said. Finally, Eva Green Benson, wife of John T. Benson, was sent by the doctors to ready Mrs. McClurkan for the end, and again Mrs. McClurkan said, "He is going to get well." And miraculously he did get well and before too long was back at work.[30]

While recovering from his illness, Brother McClurkan continued to struggle with the question of what to do with the following of holiness people in Nashville and Middle Tennessee who were looking to him for leadership. He began to see Nashville in a new way, as a center for the proclamation of holiness. Heath describes her father's reaction to Nashville: "He saw Nashville, with its favorable location, its transportation facilities, its educational structure, as a center strategic to the dissemination of scriptural holiness throughout the South. At the same time there had been growing up within him a deepening conviction that this was his field of labor. This conviction grew and abided. He could not escape it. Acting upon it, after earnest prayer for guidance, Father planted his handful of seed in the soil of Nashville, deep in the Father's will as he understood it. He immediately appointed a committee from the small following of holiness people and requested it to provide ways and means for conserving the summer's work, with the result that they secured the Conservatory of Music for temporary use, and God did the rest."[31]

Old Tulip Street Methodist Church, located on the East side of Fifth Street between Fatherland and Russell Streets (Nashville, Tennessee)

Apparently McClurkan stayed the winter of 1897-1898 in Nashville and held services for his little flock of holiness people in the Conservatory of Music building on the corner of Fifth Avenue and Cedar Street. The meetings never conflicted with the regular services of the churches to which the people belonged. Their purpose was mutual fellowship as they gathered together for prayer, praise, and preaching. While there are no records of any organization at this time, it seems that these services were the early beginnings of a sense of identity for what later came to be called the Pentecostal Tabernacle and eventually First Church of the Nazarene.

Revivals soon began to pour forth from this holiness band of workers that was said to have stirred the whole city of Nashville.[32] Meetings which lasted for several weeks were held in the Methodist churches in South Nashville and North Nashville, and many people were being saved and sanctified.[33]

It soon became evident that larger quarters than the Conservatory would be necessary to accommodate the people who were attending these services. About this time a committee of laymen from Tulip Street Methodist Church called on McClurkan and offered him the use of their old church building free of charge. McClurkan and his people would have only to make the necessary repairs and maintain its upkeep. This building, a historic landmark of distinction in Southern Methodism, was located on the east side of Fifth Street between Fatherland and Russell Streets, scarcely one hundred yards from the present site of First Church of the Nazarene at 510 Woodland Street, Nashville, Tennessee.[34]

"The Committee," the first official church board (1898) when the Pentecostal Alliance (Mission) was located on the East side of Fifth Street, between Fatherland and Russell Streets (Standing, L to R—John T. Benson, E. H. Welburn, Jim Yeaman, Tim H. Moore; seated—Arthur Ransom, J. O. McClurkan, Ed. W. Thompson)

The first recorded "Minutes" of McClurkan's holiness band, dated May 14, 1898, report the formation of a committee, probably appointed by McClurkan, consisting of six men: Arthur S. Ransom, chairman; E. H. Welburn, secretary; and John T. Benson, Ed W. Thompson, F. M. Atchison, and Robert Jackson.[35] This group had been "appointed for the purpose of taking charge of and controlling the old Tulip Street (Methodist) Church in the interest of the Holiness Movement in Nashville, Tennessee."[36] The significance of the May 14, 1898, date as a first point of official organization is noted by Millard Reed: "It could accurately be said that the very first meeting on May 14, 1898, was a small but significant step toward denominational-type organization."[37]

There were eight meetings of this committee between May 14 and June 8, 1898. The following is a brief list of some their accomplishments: (1) secured the use of the old Tulip Street Methodist Church for the holiness movement, (2) made plans for a series of tent meetings in the summer of 1898, (3) agreed to hold services at times that would not conflict with the regular services of churches to which the people belonged, (4) secured a fifty-book holiness library, (5) elected J. O. McClurkan superintendent for the holiness work in Nashville, and (6) used the name "Association," apparently thinking of itself as a renewed Holiness Association in Middle Tennessee.[38]

Leadership of J. O. McClurkan

What was it about J. O. McClurkan that would lead the Committee to elect him superintendent of the holiness work in Nashville and Middle Tennessee? For one thing, he was a deeply spiritual man and a man of prayer. Jasper White describes him as "a symbol of all that is Christian. He forever looked for the good in men."[39] Dr. C. E. Hardy in the 1946 Trevecca Founder's Day address described McClurkan: "He was a compassionate man. He was a man who sympathized with people. He seemed to have an instinct to find out about people and their troubles and to know the proper time to… tell them he was praying for them."[40]

Brother McClurkan was "very sociable and easy to approach. Everyone felt at ease in his presence…. Courtesy was one of his outstanding characteristics…. He was a man of good judgment…. He loved people."[41] Wynkoop says that McClurkan's leadership style was characterized by his "ability to lead without ostentation. There must have been a charisma about him that drew quality people to him. He led by inspiring the genius of others. He almost seemed to follow rather than lead. But he was never very far away."[42]

In a Founder's Day message at Trevecca Nazarene College in 1945, Emmett McClurkan said of his father: "He was a great man with a great soul. He was a profound thinker, a natural-born leader. People followed him. He was able to find the loose ends of a tangled life and help piece it together again. He had the common touch. He had the qualities that make for leadership."[43]

McClurkan's ability to look on the positive side of life contributed to his effective leadership. Merle McClurkan Heath states that it was her father's practice to never emphasize the negatives and to speak little of life's difficulties, as he was a man with the affirmatives of life implanted in him. She adds, "One of Father's rare qualities was the fact that he never lost the amazement at sin. Sin always surprised and perplexed him even as the years unrolled and he came to minister to so much of it in the lives of so many people—misery and crime and degradation. You see, the secret of it was that Father was never look-ing for *sin*. He was looking for the *sinner,* and the peculiarity of his vision was such that he saw beyond the sin straight into the sinner's heart and beheld there a soul worth saving, a son of God in the making."[44]

In addition to being a biblical preacher and teacher, McClurkan was a man of vision. John T. Benson Jr. describes this vision:

> He was God's man at God's appointed place, on God's time schedule to begin a great work in the city of Nashville… It is evi-dent that Brother McClurkan had a vision of being more than a pastor of the local congregation at Nashville. From the start he had plans for the spread of the Holiness Movement at home and abroad, and to this end he moved quickly. He invited the Holiness people to come together as a body for a Convention…. History must record it as the First Convention taking place in Nashville, Tennessee, convening July 18, 1898, at old Tulip Street Church at 5th and Russell Streets. The Convention took place about six weeks after Brother McClurkan's election as the superintendent.[45]

Formation of the Pentecostal Alliance

Soon after a home base was established in Nashville, McClurkan began to think about a plan to unite the holiness people in Middle Tennessee to conserve and develop the fruits of his recent revival efforts in that area. He did not feel that the battle could be perma-nently won by just going from place to place and holding a few days' meeting. Rather, he thought that the movement should be organized and missions established in the towns and cities.[47]

John T. and Eva Benson, prominent leaders in the
Pentecostal Tabernacle and Pentecostal Mission

Therefore, in midsummer of 1898, McClurkan sent out a call for the holiness people of Middle Tennessee to send representatives to a convention in Nashville for the purpose of "organizing the Holiness work into some kind of band for the promotion of God's work."[48] The Convention was held in the old Tulip Street Church, July 18-20, and the result was the creation of an organization known as the Pentecostal Alliance. The Convention elected a three-man executive committee and empowered them to select four more members. The original seven-man executive committee was composed of J. O. McClurkan, chairman and an ordained minister of the Cumberland Presbyterian Church; John T. Benson, secretary and prominent Southern Methodist layman and businessman; B. Helm, treasurer and ordained minister of the Southern Presbyterian Church; J. J. Rye, an ordained minister of the Cumberland Presbyterian Church; B. F. Haynes, ordained elder of the Southern Methodist Church and editor of *Zion's Outlook;* John Radcliffe, layman; and Arthur S. Ransom, layman who had found sanctifying grace under the preaching of McClurkan.[49]

John T. Benson Jr. gives the following description of the spiritual fervor of this first Convention in 1898 based on his reading of the "Minutes":

> This Holiness Convention of July 18 through 20 of 1898 must have given Father [John T. Benson] a witness to the fervency of shouts, testimonies, preaching, praying and singing that he had never seen before in that old church.... What a memory it must have been

> to John T. Benson, a sedate businessman, a dignified partner in the firm of Cummins, Benson and McKay and a Scottish Rite Mason.... Moreover I would suggest that Brother McClurkan, the dignified Cumberland Presbyterian, a man of the cloth with his cutaway Prince Albert coat, his high collar and string tie, in all likelihood, was as much surprised and enthralled with the fervency of that first Convention in 1898 as [was] his right hand man, John T. Benson.[50]

The choice of the name "Pentecostal Alliance" may have been suggested by the New York-based Christian and Missionary Alliance group founded by A. B. Simpson in 1881. Simpson's group preferred to be considered a movement rather than a denomination. They were more Keswick than Wesleyan in theology and were significantly influenced by the Eleventh Hour Movement. They also had a strong missionary outreach and emphasized the premillennial return of Christ. "J. O. McClurkan was so closely connected with the Christian and Missionary Alliance during an early period of his own mission," says Wynkoop, "that the two were virtually identical."[51] When the relationship ended in 1901, McClurkan's "Alliance" was changed to "Mission."

In choosing the term "Pentecostal," McClurkan adopted a term that was commonly used in the American Holiness Movement to refer to an emphasis on entire sanctification in terms of the Spirit-filled life.[52] However, as W. T. Purkiser points out, "'Pentecostal' at this period had no connotation of glossolalia or 'unknown tongues' such as it acquired later.... None of the groups which became a part of the Church of the Nazarene accepted glossolalia as a genuine spiritual gift, and the adjective 'Pentecostal' in the name of the denomination became so confusing that it was officially dropped by the General Assembly of 1919."[53] McClurkan also found it necessary to disclaim any relationship to tongues-speaking groups that used the term "Pentecostal."[54]

The goal of the Pentecostal Alliance was not to form a new denomination, but to band the holiness people of Middle Tennessee together in such a way as to best serve the Lord without breaking away from their church affiliation. In one of his early promotional circulars, McClurkan said, "We do not now, and never have advised our people to cut loose from their church memberships."[55] There was only one requirement for membership in the Alliance: "Either one professed sanctification or was seeking it. No other church affiliation needed to be broken. To this end, the Alliance welcomes to its fold all truly sanctified people, or seekers for the same, irrespective of church affiliations. Hence a man can belong to any church he pleases and at the same time be a member of the Alliance."[56]

McClurkan publicized a three-fold purpose of the Pentecostal Alliance in the September 22, 1898, issue of the paper, *Zion's Outlook:* "1. To foster the work where it is now planted, seeing that Pentecostal services are held regularly, thereby strengthening the work already begun. 2. To press onward in the evangelizing of the home field, as the Lord may direct…. 3. To kindle the flames of missionary zeal which burned on the altars of the Apostolic Church…."[57] McClurkan then added,

> We represent only a small section of the Pentecostal forces. The alliance organization originated chiefly with those who were used of the Lord to assist in opening up the work through this district. If others like the plan, and wish to join us, all right. If someone else has anything better to offer, we will unite with them. Should the time come when the churches will do this work, then we stand ready to disband. We do not want a new denomination. It seems to us we have too many already. If the time ever comes when the dear Lord wants His people to organize a new church, He will so indicate it. In the meantime let us stand in our lot and testify to His riches of grace before an unbelieving and adulterous generation, until He comes or we fall asleep in Him.[58]

This early Wesleyan Holiness Movement in Middle Tennessee was strongly independent and nondenominational. Both preachers and laymen within the movement were mainly concerned with people finding sanctifying grace and contributing to their own denominational churches. The freedom and joy experienced in their services negated the need for formal organization.

Their simple organization may be seen in John T. Benson Jr.'s summary of the accomplishments of the First Convention of July 1898:

1. The Convention adopted a name for the Holiness Movement— "The Pentecostal Alliance."
2. The Convention made its first beginning in issuing credentials to preachers and Christian workers in the name of the

Pentecostal Alliance. Notably, Thomas Banks Dean appears to have been the very first applicant receiving a certificate as a lay (evangelist) worker.

3. The Convention made its first move to establish a program for Foreign Missions. Brother Helm was instructed to investigate.

4. Made plans to form or organize Pentecostal Alliances [local congregations]. Apparently these were to be prayer bands, mission groups and circles of believers....

5. Put in motion a plan to write and adopt a set of "Rules [of Faith] and Practices" for the Pentecostal Alliance and ordered 1,000 copies to be printed for distribution.

6. The Convention elected seven good men as the Executive Committee to carry on the work.

7. The Convention provided for the ordination of preachers. The ordained elders of the Executive Committee were given the power to ordain applicants upon the recommendation of the entire Executive Committee.[59]

In Nashville, J. O. McClurkan served as pastor of the small congregation of holiness believers to whom he preached on Sunday afternoons and nights and Thursday nights. Those attending these services could go to their own local churches for Sunday school, Sunday morning services, and Wednesday night prayer services. The three services conducted by McClurkan were held in the old Tulip Street Church, except during the summer months when all gathered together in holiness tent meetings throughout the city.[60]

Growth of the Pentecostal Alliance

A second Convention of the Pentecostal Alliance was held November 23-27, 1899, in the old Tulip Street Church, with J. O. McClurkan presiding. About 100 friends and delegates attended. One of the speakers was Dr. Henry Wilson of New York, representing the Christian and Missionary Alliance. About $2,000 was raised for missions even though there was no mission program at that time. Eleven "lay evangelists" were given certificates and the Executive Committee was empowered to revise the as-yet-unapproved "rules of faith and practice" and to submit them for ratification to the several congregations composing the Alliance. In addition, an impressive healing service was conducted by Dr. Henry Wilson. Divine healing was a major emphasis of both the Pentecostal Alliance and the Christian and Missionary Alliance.[61]

Prior to the meeting of the Third Convention in November 1900, two significant events associated with the Pentecostal Alliance had taken place. One was the purchase of a religious paper, *Zion's Outlook*, an action resulting from the personal tragedy of the owner and editor, B. F. Haynes. When Haynes suffered financial loss and was unable to satisfy a $3,300 debt against the paper, McClurkan called a meeting "of the brethren interested in the holiness movement" on May 15, 1900, to consider acquiring *Zion's Outlook* for the Pentecostal Alliance. He said it would be an undenominational holiness organ that would contribute to the spread of scriptural holiness throughout the South. Three leading laymen associated with McClurkan's work came to the rescue (John T. Benson, A. S. Ransom, and Tim Moore), assumed the financial indebtedness, and brought *Zion's Outlook* under the control of the Pentecostal Alliance. McClurkan soon assumed the editorship, and this religious paper became a major tool for promoting the holiness work of the Alliance.[62]

The second event was the Lebanon, Tennessee, Camp Meeting, August 4-14, 1900. Holiness work had begun in Lebanon in 1897 through the ministry of Methodist pastor, B. F. Haynes. Also, McClurkan had held a series of meetings in and around Lebanon. A tabernacle was built there and hundreds were converted and sanctified in the revival meetings. The newspaper clippings tell that 2,500 people were present in the services on August 5 and that the services included shouting, singing, preaching, and praying—a real "freedom in the Spirit" with the absence of any fanaticism or "tongues speaking." Newspaper coverage two days before the close of the meeting said,

> Some of the toughest characters in Lebanon and Wilson Counties have been converted... church members have been warmed up and backsliders reclaimed. Forty or fifty men and women Christian workers were here from Nashville during the entire ten days helping in the meeting.... Perhaps the number of conversions will reach into the hundreds and many were blessed being sanctified....

No one can fail to observe that all the great revivals nowadays are Holiness meetings…. This is a religious work which the regular denominational and orthodox churches had failed to accomplish with all their machinery and money. These… men and women, filled with the power of the Holy Spirit, did more in four years than had been previously done in twenty-five.[63]

The Third Annual Convention of the Pentecostal Alliance was held November 15-20, 1900, in the newly acquired Hynes School Building at Fifth and Jo Johnston Avenues north of the State Capitol building, with over 125 delegates from some nine states and nine denominations. The Alliance had outgrown the old Tulip Street Church facilities and had purchased the Hynes building in 1900 for the sum of $5,000.[64]

Several Christian and Missionary Alliance personnel were present at this third Convention and served as main speakers, indicating the close relationship between the two bodies. Between $2,500 and $3,000 was raised for foreign missions, and W. A. Farmer, a Vanderbilt University student from Covington, Georgia, was appointed the first Pentecostal Alliance missionary to China. Since the Pentecostal Alliance had no mission board and no experience in sending out missionaries to foreign lands, the Convention decided to send Farmer under the Christian and Missionary Alliance organization in New York.[65]

The year 1901 was a pivotal year in the life of the Pentecostal Alliance under the leadership of J. O. McClurkan.[66] In its February 11, 1901, meeting, the Pentecostal Alliance General Committee ordained its first minister, John L. Boaze, by the "laying on of hands."[67] In August the same committee discussed charges of "certain Texas brethren" against the character of an Alliance brother, H. O. Moore. J. O. McClurkan and J. J. Rye went to Texas to check out this problem, but the accusers withdrew their charges before a church trial could be arranged.[68] The Alliance was thus assuming responsibility for its leaders and involving itself in ecclesiastical matters with its ordination of ministers and certificates for evangelists and Christian workers, even to the point of possible discipline. By then the Alliance had purchased property in Lebanon for the annual camp meeting. The newly acquired Hynes Building housed the central headquarters of the Alliance and the office of *Zion's Outlook*. Sometime in 1901, John T. Benson resigned his lucrative position as partner in Cummins, Benson, and McKay wholesale brokerage business to become associated with J. O. McClurkan on a full-time basis.[69]

*Old Hynes School building, birthplace of the Bible Training School,
acquired by the Pentecostal Alliance in 1900, located at Fifth Avenue
and Jo Johnston Street north of the State Capitol*

The most significant event of 1901 was the Fourth Annual Convention held October 30-November 4. There were 125 delegates attending from several states and six denominations. Encouraging reports were given by the Alliance workers from the various sections of the Southeast. There was an outpouring of the Holy Spirit reflected in the preaching, praying, singing, and testifying. In the business session, it was decided to change the name of the interdenominational fellowship from Pentecostal Alliance to Pentecostal Mission and to place its management under a General Committee of twenty-five members, subdivided into a Home Mission Committee and Foreign Missionary Bureau with an Executive Committee for each one.[70] The change in name suggests a drawing back from a possible union with A. B. Simpson's Christian and Missionary Alliance.[71] The November 4, 1901, Executive Committee "Minutes" indicate a discontinuation of supporting and sending missionaries other than those sent out by the Pentecostal Mission.[72] Wynkoop concludes that the Pentecostal Mission had now "severed official connection with the Christian and Missionary Alliance and no longer sent either funds or missionary trainees to the headquarters in Nyack, New York. The Mission was more 'on its own' than it ever considered being in its more idealistic days."[73] Even though the Pentecostal Mission was no longer affiliated with the Christian and Missionary Alliance, there was evidently no break in fellowship and no personality clash. McClurkan declared that his people still felt "close kinship to and love for that devout people."[74]

The Annual Convention of 1901 described the mission of the body: "To seek the salvation of the lost; the sanctification of believers; the deepening of the spiritual life; and the dissemination of Scriptural knowledge of the Lord."[75] In addition, a confession of faith was spelled out in the following summary of doctrinal beliefs:

1. The verbal inspiration of the Bible.
2. The Trinity of the Godhead.
3. The total depravity of the Human Race through the fall.
4. The vicarious atonement of Jesus Christ.
5. A future state of undying blessedness for the saved and unending conscious suffering for the lost.
6. Repentance, regeneration, justification by faith in Christ; sanctification for the believer obtainable in this life, through faith in the blood of Jesus Christ and the personal indwelling of the Holy Spirit; the healing of the bodies of believers by Jesus Christ in answer to the prayer of faith; the premillennial coming of our Lord and Savior Jesus Christ to reign on earth as King; the obligation of the Great Commission resting on every believer: "Go ye into all the world and preach the Gospel to every creature." [76]

Eligibility for membership in the Pentecostal Mission was now based on agreement with these doctrinal beliefs and the "satisfactory evidence of personal salvation."[77]

The 1901 Convention also included rules for organizational changes which Wynkoop says "actually constituted the Mission a virtual denomination."[78] This organizational structure included such churchly features as the General Committee of twenty-five members to be elected annually by the Mission and reporting to it each year, the Home Missions and Foreign Missions Committees, and the appointment of five district superintendents for the Home Mission work: J. J. Rye, Clarksville District; H. G. Rogers, Columbia District; J. L. Boaze, Murfreesboro District; W. A. Hughes, Clifton District; and C. S. Bruner, Cordova, Alabama, District.[79] Moreover, careful rules were set up to guide the financial aspects of the Pentecostal Mission. While missionaries were not pledged a salary, there was some financial support for the following six missionaries in 1901:

W. A. Farmer, South China

John E. Fee, South China

Mrs. Annie Lewis, Sudan

Mrs. Arthur Williams, Congo Free State

Mr. And Mrs. William Ramsey, India[80]

Two other events of 1901 seem worthy of note. One was the starting of Sunday school and Sunday morning services at McClurkan's holiness tabernacle in Nashville early that year. This full schedule of three Sunday services may have "constrained people to give up their own churches," says Benson.[81] The other major event of 1901 was McClurkan's starting a series of Bible classes at night for his adult workers during the winter months of 1900–1901. These classes culminated in the founding of a Bible Training School in November of 1901, the forerunner of Trevecca Nazarene University.[82]

During the three and one-half years since the formation of the Pentecostal Alliance, J. O. McClurkan's movement had expanded to several southeastern states, had missionaries in several countries, and had laid the foundation for what is known today as the First Church of the Nazarene in Nashville, Tennessee, and the Tennessee District Church of the Nazarene. "Certainly, Brother McClurkan and his associates," says Benson, "had every right to feel that God's guiding hand was leading them to great accomplishments in the work of the Kingdom."[83] Merle McClurkan Heath sees her father's inspiration behind much of the accomplishments of the Pentecostal Mission: "Truly it can be told that the inspiration behind it, and all that was accomplished by it, was Father's great spirit. Its small beginning with all it came to be in the ensuing years, its developments, its enlargements, its ramifications, was largely the product of his spiritual illumination, his over-all vision for the work of the Kingdom, and his consecration to that work. His brilliant love for God and man was the root from which sprang the many branches of the work, expressing and defining, as they did, the catholicity of his outreaching interests."[84]

From 1901 to 1907, the Pentecostal Mission under the leadership of J. O. McClurkan continued to grow numerically and spiritually, including the expansion of missionary work in Cuba (1901), China (1901), Guatemala (1901), India (1903), Bolivia (1906), and Argentina (1906). By 1903 there were Pentecostal Missions in at least twenty-six locations in the State of Tennessee alone: Nashville, Keser's Chapel near Clarksville, Murfreesboro, Clifton, Fayetteville, Columbia, Franklin, Faxon, Enlow, Cookeville, Caney Springs, Everglade, Lebanon, Clarksville, Shiloh, Liberty, Trenton, Monterey, McEwen, Big Sandy, Kedron, Yellow Creek, Lone Oak, Liverwort, Manchester, and Chattanooga.[85] There were other missions scattered about in the adjacent states of the South.

Organizational trends continued with the incorporation of the Pentecostal Mission under the state laws of Tennessee in 1902 and the founding of the Pentecostal Mission Publishing Company in the same year (later known as the John T. Benson Publishing Company).

The publishing company resulted from McClurkan's efforts to support his family. It appears that J. O. McClurkan never received a regular salary for his services either as pastor, superintendent, editor, or college president. He was a marvelous example of dedication and self-sacrifice. Salary and security had been cast aside when he agreed to stay in Nashville in 1898. Disinterested in possessions or material gains, he was supported by freewill offerings from his preaching and from the Annual Conventions. His daughter, Merle McClurkan Heath, reports that he also supported himself by means of his book business.[86] Calling his business the Pentecostal Book and Tract Depository, McClurkan carried this "business" in a plain, split-bottom market basket containing books, tracts, and hand-embossed scripture mottoes which preached a short sermon to the purchaser, such as

"God Bless This Home," "Jesus Saves," "God Is Love," "Prayer Changes Things." Benson says, "Out of the proceeds of these sales came the extra money for Brother McClurkan's support for his family, and at the same time he was ministering to people with books, tracts, and mottoes."[87] And out of this "basket" development came the Pentecostal Mission Publishing Company which, under the management of John T. Benson, not only published *Zion's Outlook* but also housed the Book and Tract Depository. Heath observes, "Here the choicest literature produced within the ranks of the Holiness Movement could be secured, as well as the best devotional literature in the religious field, together with tracts and mottoes and Bibles."[88]

In 1903 the name of the weekly paper edited by McClurkan was changed from *Zion's Outlook* to *Living Water.* The "Minutes" of the Pentecostal Mission do not explain why this change was made. The idea to change the name may have come from S. C. Todd and J. M. Pike who were editing an independent weekly paper from Atlanta, Georgia, with the name of *Living Water,* and who along with others from the Southeast, united with the Pentecostal Alliance (Mission) in September 1901.[89] Since *Zion's Outlook* and *Living Water* were going to many of the same people and doing the same work, it would appear that some mutual arrangement was worked out between the friends, McClurkan, Todd, and Pike. As a result of the union, in January 1903 McClurkan's *Zion's Outlook* became *Living Water.*[90] Although the paper had been taken for granted as a semi-official organ of the Pentecostal Mission, the 1904 Annual Convention voted to adopt *Living Water* as its official paper.[91]

In 1905 the Pentecostal Mission moved to a new location on Fourth Avenue North between Broadway and Commerce Streets near the Ryman Auditorium.[92] This building would provide adequate room for the Pentecostal Tabernacle, printing and book departments, parsonage quarters, and Bible Training School. The Eighth Annual Convention was held in these new facilities October 6-9, 1905. For the first time a yearbook was to be published describing the year's activities of the missions, districts, committees, missionaries, pastors, and evangelists.[93] Unfortunately, no copies of this first yearbook have been preserved, according to this writer's research.

The 1906 Annual Convention which met October 4-8 faced four

major problems. One was the relationship between the Pentecostal Mission and the local bodies of holiness bands. After rejecting a committee recommendation to develop a "plan of church organization" which would have given the Pentecostal Mission the status of a denomination, the Convention accepted the following substitute motion made by John T. Benson: "Inasmuch as a number of congregations have already been formed among our mission people, and there is a growing demand still for others, we would recommend that wherever such congregations are formed, if they so desire, they may come under the care of the Pentecostal Mission and may be supplied thereby as far as possible with the ministry of the Word. In other words, these local congregations may become a part of the Pentecostal Mission, just as a prayer band or a local mission."[94]

Evidently the Convention of 1906 was not yet ready to assume the disciplines of a denominational status for pastors, evangelists, missionaries, property, trusteeship, supervision, and budget assessments. "After all, the Pentecostal (Alliance) Mission was only eight years old," says John T. Benson Jr., and "Brother McClurkan believed that the Holiness Movement was a *fellowship* of believers committed to work through various denominations."[95]

A second problem the 1906 Convention faced was the problem of issuing certificates or credentials to ordained ministers, evangelists, and lay workers. While there seems to have been discussion of possibly doing away with certificates for lay workers, the decision was to continue all three types of certificates for ordained ministers, evangelists, and lay workers. However, the following four requirements were outlined as conditions for receiving a certificate: 1. Must be of good Christian experience and character, 2. Must agree doctrinally with the Pentecostal Mission beliefs, 3. Must give an annual report to the Convention either in person or in writing, and 4. Must make proper effort to advance the work of the Pentecostal Mission and its branches.[96]

The third problem had to do with the ordination of women. It was well known that Brother McClurkan was willing for women to be preachers, evangelists, missionaries, and teachers, but that he did not believe that women should be ordained for ruling positions. McClurkan's position on the ordination of women was one of his differences with Dr. Bresee and the Nazarenes as reflected in their correspondence in 1907.[97] The Convention finally concluded that the Scriptures did permit women to preach and hold meetings but that the ordination of women was not deemed to be scriptural.[98]

The fourth problem that faced the young holiness movement was the relationship of missionaries on the field to the Pentecostal Mission. Much progress had been made on the mission fields by the dedicated missionaries now serving under the banner of the Pentecostal Mission. However, there had also been some problems and concerns. The committee appointed to study the problem presented the following recommendation to the Convention, a recommendation which was adopted:

> Missionaries on the field shall be responsible to the Pentecostal Mission as respects their moral conduct, their doctrinal views, and the administration of their mission work…. In the organization of mission churches they are to be organized in the simplest form of church government found in the New Testament and they are to adhere as far as possible to Biblical names for the church and her officers… and that our missionaries hold such relation to the native churches as the evangelists of the New Testament did. We also recommend that in the ordination of native church officers as deacons, elders, evangelists, pastors, and teachers, the power of ordination be exercised… with the foreign elders jointly….[99]

The Tenth Annual Convention of the Pentecostal Mission in early October 1907 was the "most successful ever held in the history of the work," according to the *Living Water* issue of October 17, 1907. There was a large number of delegates from various states, and at times the crowds were too great to be accommodated. The spirit of the Convention was fervently missionary, and the gospel song "I'm Going Through" was first introduced to the 1907 Holiness Convention. Mention was made of the Pentecostal Mission's new facility, the Training Home for Girls (orphanage) located at the north end of McFerrin Avenue in East Nashville. A highlight of the Convention was the annual message of J. O. McClurkan on "burden-bearing and a passion for others" which was "powerfully blessed of the Lord." *Living Water* (October 17, 1907) reported that, as the Convention closed, "delegates and other attendants returned to their work with a wider vision, nobler purpose, and a deeper love for the perishing than ever before and with a feeling in the heart that God had led throughout."

The 1907 Annual Convention "Minutes" record the first mention of the Nazarenes in an announcement by Brother McClurkan that the group was invited to attend in Chicago a meeting of the Church of the Nazarene from the West and the Association of Pentecostal Churches of America from the East beginning on October 10, 1907. The Convention voted that Brother McClurkan appoint a Committee to attend.[100] This invitation was the culmination of the correspondence between McClurkan and the Nazarenes that had occurred during 1907. This story will be picked up in a later section of this chapter, "The Issue of Denominationalism."

Bible Training School/Trevecca College

"I did not start Trevecca on my own. It was thrust upon me in the Providence of the Lord."[101]

J. O. McClurkan

THE ORIGINS OF TREVECCA NAZARENE UNIVERSITY GO BACK TO TWO major sources: (1) A *pastor's class* started by J. O. McClurkan in the winter months of 1900–1901 for the training of his adult workers.[102] This program consisted of a series of evening Bible classes and personal evangelism. According to Heath, the first class consisted of about eight students, including Mr. and Mrs. John T. Benson, Mr. and Mrs. E. H. Welburn, and members of McClurkan's church board.[103] This small pastor's class grew rapidly, and soon other classes were started with additional teachers. (2) *A need for trained Christian workers for both the home and foreign fields,* including pastors, evangelists, missionaries, and lay workers. "The growth of the missionary program and the expanding influence of the Pentecostal Mission caused a need for trained Christian workers," says Eugene Williams in his unpublished thesis on the "History of Trevecca Nazarene College."[104] "The Pentecostal Alliance was not put together specifically to found a school," says Wynkoop, "but the need for trained Christian ministers [and missionaries] became a major issue as the work grew and young people were asking to be sent to foreign fields."[105]

On March 7, 1901, when the separation from the Christian and Missionary Alliance was foreseen, McClurkan ran an announcement in *Zion's Outlook* that a "Bible Training School" would open in the fall. The "philosophy" of the school was expressed in the lead article, a review of F. L. Chappell's *The Eleventh Hour Laborers:* "Bible Institutes and training schools are among the products of the eleventh hour movement. There is an open door for such an institution in this city, and if the Lord so directs, we will begin the work this fall."[106]

Wynkoop believes that this early announcement of a school and the lead article on the "Eleventh Hour Movement" reflect McClurkan's early thinking on the kind of institution he envisioned, the theology behind it, the method of financing it, and its nondenominational stance. She claims that the roots of his educational philosophy can be traced to several sources, including "Cumberland Presbyterianism, the Holiness Movement, the Prophetic Bible Conference movement, Keswick teaching, the Christian and Missionary Alliance groups as well as Methodistic traces."[107]

During the next few months as plans were made for the courses of study, a broader concept of Christian education seems to emerge and is reflected in McClurkan's announcement in the May 30, 1901, issue of *Zion's Outook* in an article entitled "Bible Training School":

> We are planning to open a Bible Training School here next fall. There is a wide field for such work. Many persons who feel distinctly called to missionary, evangelistic, and other branches of Christian work, are unable to take a thorough college course, but they can avail themselves of a shorter and more practical course of study. The courses will be eclectic, allowing the students to pursue such studies as will be most helpful, such as practical English, Historical and Mathematical studies, together with the Holy Scriptures. Those who choose to do so can study the Bible in the original languages, Greek and Hebrew, under efficient instruction. Another valuable feature will be the practical work in which the many methods and phases of the most successful religious work will be discussed. The pupils will be in constant touch with open air meetings, missions, and other kinds of evangelistic services. The practical knowledge derived therefrom will be invaluable.

Nashville enjoys the reputation of being the "Athens of the South," and we want to see a school in this great educational and religious center where the full gospel can be taught, without limit or restriction. To this end, let all our co-workers join us in prayer that God may mightily prosper the enterprise. There is ample room in the third story of our present headquarters for quite a large school.[108]

In August 1901, a further clarification of the curriculum is announced by McClurkan under the title "Eclectic." Analyzing this statement, Wynkoop observes that "one feels that McClurkan's Presbyterian conviction about a properly trained ministry is prevailing over the Eleventh Hour haste and willingness to settle for the educational shortcut."[109] The announcement stated that

Competent teachers will be secured. It is our purpose to select just such a course of Bible study as will best qualify Christian workers for soul winning. Many of our people need this training. In addition to Bible study, the following English and classical courses can be taken, if desired:

1. Spelling. Webster's Primary Dictionary.
2. Reading. Revised Readers.
3. Grammar. Harvey's Revised.
4. Arithmetic. Ray's New Practical.
5. Writing. Serial Copy Books.
6. Mathematics. Geometry, Algebra, Higher Arithmetic.
7. English. Higher English, Grammar, and Rhetoric.
8. Greek. Some parts of New Testament in Greek, with Greek Grammar.
9. Latin.
10. Hebrew or Sacred History.
11. General Reviews [over their studies] Given in January and April.[110]

The Pentecostal Literary and Bible Training School formally opened on November 5, 1901, the day after the close of the Fourth Annual Convention, in the Pentecostal Alliance Headquarters Building (old Hynes School) with twenty-five students, the first one of whom was William M. Tidwell.[111] According to Heath, tuition was *free* and room and board was $10.00 a month. McClurkan's open door invitation stated, "And if you do not have that, preacher boy, come on anyway. Together we will find a way."[112] J. O. McClurkan acted as president and dean. Mrs. J. O. McClurkan said that her husband had the idea, "He (God) and I are running the school, others are helpers."[113]

At this stage the school was not open to the general public, but only to those who were preparing for some specific area of Christian service. The length of the school term was six months, with an extended time for personal evangelism in the summer. Entrance requirements were very simple, based on personal dedication to God and a sense of call to Christian service. No denominational affiliation was necessary. Most students were poor and had to work to attend school.[114]

"J. O. McClurkan was a genius in the way that he financed the Pentecostal Mission and the Bible Training School," states Benson.[115] He had no financial backing except for his friends and his faith that God would supply the needs. "This attitude reflects his 'Eleventh Hour' philosophy. [His friends]… were 'holding up his hands' as Moses' hands were held up because they believed in the man and what he was doing," says Wynkoop.[116] *Zion's Outlook,* and later *Living Water,* included reminders and even pleas for contributions for the needs of the school.

During the first few years of the Bible Training School, distinguishing the Training School from the Pentecostal Mission was difficult. The same "General Committee" directed both. Wynkoop suggests that the relationship of the Training School to the Mission was analogous to a Sunday school's relationship to the church that runs it.[117]

The faculty of the Bible Training School was composed of dedicated teachers who probably received little or no salary during the first few years of the school. Among those who made both class work and field education exciting for the students was Miss Henrietta Matson, a former missionary to Africa and India who had been educated in Scotland. She also held the chair of mathematics at Fisk University in Nashville and gave the rest of her time to McClurkan's Bible Training School. She was competent in Greek and mathematics and instilled a deep interest in missions in her students. "She was a walking encyclopedia of information," says Heath, "as well as a boiling spirit for missions, and her godly influence and ability were

God-given boons in those initial months of Trevecca."[118] Another early faculty member was Miss Fannie Claypool who arrived unannounced from Virginia to offer her services to the Bible School and became a beloved English teacher as well as office editor of *Living Water.*

From an advertisement in *Zion's Outlook* in 1902 announcing the opening of school that fall, seven faculty men and women were identified as instructors: (1) J. O. McClurkan (Bible, theology, biblical history, general history), (2) Elmer E. Van Ness (grammar, physics, physical geography), (3) E. C. Sanders (arithmetic, physiology, geography), (4) Miss Mattie Staley (U.S. history, rhetoric and composition, spelling), (5) Mrs. A. S. Ransom (voice culture, reading, literature), (6) E. H. Welburn (vocal music), (7) Mrs. John T. Benson (instrumental music). Greek and Spanish were also listed but no instructors were named.[119]

*The Bible School student body in front of the
Fourth Avenue North Tabernacle (probably 1907)*

In this same advertisement in 1902, the purpose of the Bible Training School was described: "to better equip for the home and foreign field Christian men and women who need and desire a better knowledge of God's Word…. The Bible Training School, at Nashville, is the result of a long-felt need." Although tuition was free, regular board in the Mission building with J. O. McClurkan's family was $10.00 per month, and board in the dormitory was $6.00 per month.[120]

At the close of each school year, Brother McClurkan held evangelistic campaigns all over the Southeast. These services helped to attract new students and the school grew steadily. By the 1904–1905 session there were seventy students enrolled.[121] Due to the growth of both Mission and Bible School, in 1905 it became necessary to move to a new location at 125 Fourth Avenue North (between Broadway and Commerce Streets) behind the Ryman Auditorium. By the opening of school in the fall of 1905, a new three-story brick building was ready, 173 feet long and 70 feet wide, equipped with electric lights, bathrooms, laundry, dustless blackboards, maps, instruments, and other modern accessories.[122] The Pentecostal Tabernacle occupied the street floor. The parsonage was on the second floor, and the Bible School occupied the remainder of the second floor and all of the third floor.

This move downtown put the Mission and the school at the "cross-roads of Nashville life."[123] Wynkoop notes another significance to this move: It "marked another 'birthday' for the school, in a sense. For the first time the school was an entity to be considered and to be required to assume responsibilities. Its growing size and importance to the Mission made a change of location imperative. The school did not follow the Mission but the Mission, now, needed to follow the school."[124]

While McClurkan never lost the urgency of the Eleventh Hour Movement, he continued to expand his educational vision. He announced an enlargement of course offerings in the September 1905 issue of *Living Water* that included "a common English Course and a Normal Course for those who would expect to spend part of their time in teaching. [These courses] include nearly all the subjects taught in our first-class colleges."[125] McClurkan wanted to keep the school in the "Athens of the South" because he thought keeping the school in Nashville would "not only be a blessing to the city, but will be a distributing point from which hundreds of trained workers will be sent for the evangelization of the world."[126] By the end of the 1905–1906 school session, there were over eighty students representing about fifteen denominations.[127]

During these years the Bible Training School never wavered from its nondenominational stance, a position that is reflected in the *Living Water* issue of September 14, 1905: "The school is strictly nonsectarian in character. It is run in the interest of no particular church. Denominational lines are not drawn. Christ is exalted rather than a sect. None need have any fear of an effort being made to proselyte them. We are one in Jesus." The theologically eclectic spirit of J. O. McClurkan is seen in his intention to promote the "advantageous points in both the Calvinistic and Arminian systems of theology."[128] The adoption in 1910 of the name "Trevecca" for the school is another indication of that eclectic spirit.

Trevecca College

As students were finishing the school work offered by the Pentecostal Literary and Bible Training School, many expressed a desire for regular college training from McClurkan and his faculty. In response, the Bible Training School became "Trevecca College for Christian Workers" in 1910. This change involved offering a four-year college program leading to a bachelor's degree, based on the four-year standard of the University of Tennessee.[129] In addition, the *Living Water* issue of November 10, 1910, announced an enlarged curriculum for the college that included not only the regular literary, scientific, and

Trevecka College, Wales, founded by Lady Huntingdon in 1768

classical courses that were typical of a college, but also listed a two-year medical course for missionaries and a course in nursing with lectures to be given by capable physicians of Nashville. This same announcement also described a new theological course as "comprehensive and practical" based on "Bible teaching that is dispensational, topical, doctrinal, practical, and spiritual." To accommodate the growing school, a new three-story brick building was added adjacent to the existing structure on Fourth Avenue North behind the Ryman Auditorium.

The name "Trevecca" was taken from an earlier school by that name started by Lady Huntingdon in Wales in 1768 during the Evangelical Revival in England and Wales. "The word Trevecca in Welsh is… a combination of the two words —*Tref* and *Becca*—which means the Home of Rebecca," a reference to a Rebecca Prosser who restored a medieval castle in 1578, made it her home, and named it Trevecka.[130] Based on the derivation of the name "Rebecca," the literal meaning of the word "Trevecca" is "a binding together in love."[131]

Lady Huntingdon had been converted during the Evangelical Revival and developed a close friendship with both John Wesley and George Whitefield.[132] In the 1740s, theological differences emerged between Wesley and Whitefield, resulting in two wings of the revival: "An Arminian wing led by John and Charles Wesley who preached free grace for all mankind, and a Calvinistic wing led by George Whitefield [and Howell Harris] who preached free grace, but who believed only those who had been predestined by divine decree could or would respond to God's free offer and be saved."[133] Thus the Methodist movement became divided into Wesleyan Methodists and Calvinistic Methodists. Lady Huntingdon eventually sided with Whitefield and Harris and the Calvinistic wing of Methodism, although she remained a close friend of the Wesleys.

As a woman of great means and vision, Lady Huntingdon saw the need to start a college for the training of the ministry in England and Wales "where she hoped the followers of Whitefield and Wesley might study together and bury their disagreements over grace and free will."[134] The original Trevecka College opened with seven students on August 24, 1768, on Lady Huntingdon's sixty-first birthday, in the old, refurbished Trevecka Castle. John Fletcher, the saintly and scholarly Methodist follower of John Wesley, was chosen as the first president of Trevecka, and George Whitefield preached the opening convocation sermon. William Williams's famous hymn, "Guide Me, O Thou Great Jehovah," was sung that morning. The next year John Wesley preached the first anniversary sermon. Students were given free tuition, room, and board for the three-year course as well as a new suit of clothes every year. Subjects taught were grammar, logic, Bible, rhetoric, church history, natural philosophy, geography, and many classes in practical divinity and biblical languages.[135]

Lady Huntingdon (in middle age), founder of Trevecka College in 1768

Evidently J. O. McClurkan knew about the original Trevecka in South Wales and its attempt to bridge the theological differences between Wesley and Whitefield, between Arminianism and Calvinism. "He may have read John Wesley's *Journal* and *Letters* which contain numerous references to Trevecka," observes William Greathouse.[136] At any rate, S. W. Strickland, a student of McClurkan at the time, concludes: "Knowing something of the original Trevecca College, its founder, its spirit and purpose as established by Lady Huntingdon, and after consulting in the company of Dr. C. E. Hardy and with some Methodist authorities in Nashville, Tennessee, Bro. McClurkan decided to adopt the name Trevecca for his new college. Thus the second Trevecca College was established in 1910 in Nashville, Tennessee, U.S.A. Well do I remember when this change was made. This change was the beginning of a new educational era for the school."[137]

Dr. C. E. Hardy apparently played a significant role in developing the new curriculum adopted in 1910. Having studied medicine at the University of Tennessee in Memphis, Hardy had come to Nashville to continue his medical studies at Vanderbilt University and had become a part-time teacher for McClurkan in the Bible Training School in 1908. It is very likely that Hardy suggested the adding of the medical courses.[138] *The Thirteenth Annual Bulletin of Trevecca College* (1913–1914) states that the two-year medical course and nurses' training course for missionaries were added, not to give a medical degree but to "enable missionaries to take care of themselves and others in the absence of regular physicians." In connection with the expanded curriculum, a Trevecca Hospital was established for the purpose of training nurses and medical missionaries with Dr. Hardy serving as superintendent. The hospital was located at 125 Eighth

Coleg Trefeca, as it is today in Wales, operating as the laity center for the Presbyterian Church of Wales (Calvinistic Methodism), founded in 1842 and tracing its roots back to Howell Harris— This institution is a separate Trevecka College, not associated with the Trevecka College started by Lady Huntingdon in 1768.

Avenue South, in an old southern mansion. It was advertised in the *Living Water* issue of February 12, 1914, as having "rates [that] are quite reasonable and the medical attention competent and thorough. Those desiring hospital treatment where they may be under home-like and quiet religious surroundings will find this an agreeable place." Unfortunately, the hospital venture was short-lived, for following McClurkan's death in September 1914, the hospital was closed because of a financial burden, and the equipment was exchanged for stock in Trinity Hospital on Eighth Avenue and Union Street, the forbear of today's Baptist Hospital.[139]

The new theological statement advertised in the November 10, 1910, issue of *Living Water* regarding Bible teaching as "dispensational" put McClurkan's group at odds with much of the holiness movement. As Wynkoop observes, "The Bible as interpreted *dispensationally…* puts the school [on] a different 'wave length' than the Holiness Movement generally. The Holiness Association listed the 'second coming of Christ' in its statement of faith but refused to speculate on any theory about the Advent or to define any position regarding it as a basis for fellowship. 'Dispensationalism' also made union with the Church of the Nazarene difficult because Bresee felt that theories about the details of Christ's return were not in any way essential to holiness."[140]

Pentecostal Tabernacle and Trevecca College students and faculty, 1910 or 1911

With a new name, a new curriculum, and a new building, the next step was to secure official recognition by the State of Tennessee. Consequently, a charter of incorporation was drawn up and confirmed on May 5, 1911, giving Trevecca College "the powers to confer degrees, and to do all things necessary… [for] the establishment … and maintenance of the college…." It was signed by the five original members of the Board of Trustees of Trevecca College which included J. O. McClurkan, Emmett McClurkan, John T. Benson, Ed W. Thompson, and C. E. Hardy. This step was the first in the long, fifty-eight-year quest for full accreditation.[141]

The student body continued a steady growth pattern in those early years. In 1908 there were ninety-five students from fifteen states representing ten denominations.[142] In November 1911, there were 110 students and twenty teachers at the college, with thirty more students

*Trevecca students in a holiday mood going on a picnic in a
"hired transportation vehicle"*

anticipated before the end of the year.[143] The 1912–1913 school year
showed 155 students, and by 1913–1914, the enrollment had increased
to 180 students with about three-fourths of them preparing for religious work.[144] Some of the increase in 1913 may have come from a
more open enrollment policy which stated, "Any Christian young man
or woman who wishes further equipment for life's work is eligible for
admission."[145]

The Gospel Wagon used by the students in evangelistic outreach

Along with their classroom work, Trevecca students were actively
engaged in Christian service in the Nashville area, going to jails and

hospitals, work houses and orphanages, and holding street meetings. Some of the holiness people in Nashville helped them to get a horse-drawn "Gospel Wagon" to ride to places where the streetcars could not take them.[146] On Monday evenings students gathered for the literary societies where they engaged in lively debates and exercises on subjects in history, social issues, or religious problems. This activity developed into what came to be called the Octavian Society.[147]

By 1914 the College had outgrown the Fourth Avenue property and facilities. In addition, parts of the Tabernacle and College quarters were condemned by a city fire code official, a Mr. James H. Yeaman, a former member of the Pentecostal Mission.[148] McClurkan had negotiated for the eighty-acre Percy Warner estate on Gallatin Road in East Nashville which offered ample room for future growth and expansion. The price paid for the estate was about $60,000. It included the

Trevecca's new campus off Gallatin Road in East Nashville
—The Percy Warner estate mansion

antebellum Warner mansion which would serve as the main building for the school. Fifteen acres fronting on the main highway were set aside for the school campus while the remainder was divided into building lots known as the "Trevecca Subdivision" and sold to Trevecca faculty and friends who wanted to live near the campus. The surrounding streets were later named to honor those whose lives were significant to the holiness work: McClurkan Avenue named for J. O. McClurkan; Emmett Avenue named for Brother McClurkan's only son, Emmett; Strouse Avenue named for a well-known holiness preacher of that day from Virginia; Brasher Avenue named for a close friend of McClurkan and a leading holiness Methodist preacher of

The faculty and students of Trevecca College in 1911

North Alabama; and Trevecca Avenue named for the College. In addition to its being on a main transportation route linking Chicago, Louisville, and Florida, the new campus was an ideal location for a camp meeting. Consequently, a holiness camp meeting was scheduled to be held each year on a plot of ground on the campus designated for this purpose. Outstanding holiness preachers came to Nashville to preach in these camp meetings.[149]

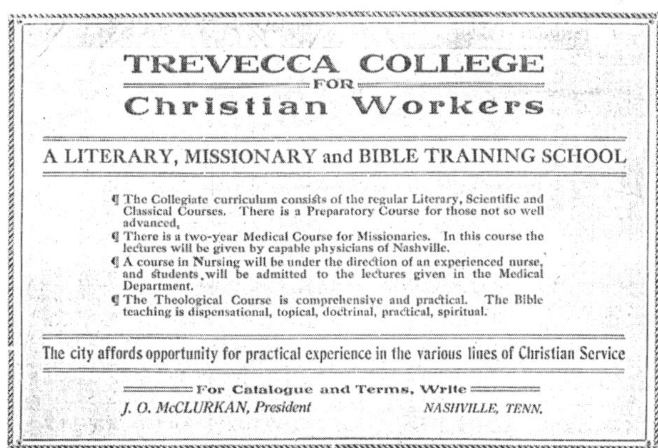

An advertisement for Trevecca College in Living Water *(about 1912)*

According to Wynkoop, this move had larger implications: "For the first time, the College was to be severed from the close family ties of the Pentecostal Mission. It was beginning to feel its own identity."[150] The Tabernacle and Mission continued to stay at the Fourth

Avenue downtown location until after it was united with the Church of the Nazarene. In 1917 it was moved back to the same East Nashville neighborhood where it had originated in 1898, a location now known as 510 Woodland Street, and became what is now Nashville First Church of the Nazarene.

Unfortunately, the day that Trevecca College was to open at the new campus in September of 1914, its beloved founder and president died of typhoid fever in St. Thomas Hospital at the young age of fifty-two. McClurkan's death will be discussed later, and the story of the College will be picked up again at the close of the next section of this chapter, "The Issue of Denominationalism."

First Church of the Nazarene in 1917 at
510 Woodland Street in Nashville, Tennessee

The Issue of Denominationalism

FROM 1907 TO 1915, THE QUESTION OF UNION WITH OTHER HOLINESS groups, including the Nazarenes, was prominent in the minds of J. O. McClurkan and his associates. "The Pentecostal Mission had from the beginning been in touch with the leaders of those holiness movements in Tennessee, Arkansas, and Texas which finally cast their lot with the Church of the Nazarene," observes Timothy Smith.[151] McClurkan was one of the evangelists at the large Waco, Texas, camp meeting in 1901 and praised the Texans for the absence of any "argumentative, bitter, censorious spirit," in spite of the severe trials through which they had passed.[152] Lasting friendships were established between McClurkan and holiness leaders in Texas, including C. B. Jernigan, R. M. Guy, A. M. Hills, and B. W. Huckabee.[153]

Members of the New Testament Church of Christ in West Tennessee were regular readers of McClurkan's weekly paper, *Zion's Outlook,* and contributed money for his missionaries. Delegates from the Pentecostal Mission attended meetings of the Arkansas Council of the Holiness Church of Christ in 1905 and expressed interest in a possible union. In 1906 R. B. Mitchum, former president of the Council of the New Testament Church of Christ, moved to Nashville and began attending McClurkan's Pentecostal Tabernacle. "Alike in basic doctrines, heirs of the same tradition of independency, and faced with the same need for organization, McClurkan and Mitchum might well have united to promote the merger of their two churches. But such was not to be," concludes Timothy L. Smith.[154]

J. O. McClurkan appears to have been well informed about the early developments of the Church of the Nazarene started by Phineas F. Bresee in Los Angeles, California, in 1895. "Nazarene preachers had come into the mid-South and warm friendships had united the hearts of McClurkan and some of these men. Many times revival meetings were conducted with McClurkan and Nazarene evangelists preaching together," writes Wynkoop.[155]

McClurkan seems to have made the first overture toward possible union with the Nazarenes in a letter written to Dr. Bresee on January 1, 1907.[156] In that letter he says,

> We have longed to see a movement of sufficient breadth and spiritual force to embrace the Pentecostal people of the different temperaments and denominational bias. We have been looking around for other kindred spirits with whom we might affiliate in such an organization. The Church of the Nazarene comes nearer our ideal than any other which we know and yet there may be difficulties that would not be easily removed in the way of our union. We like your spirit and we long for a larger fellowship with those engaged in a similar work with us. We represent quite an interest and could set in order a goodly number of congregations

in a short while were we so disposed…. We have been held together chiefly as an inspiration and fellowship rather than by organization.
But it seems to us now that we are at the parting of the way and
that we must either affiliate with the most spiritual organizations
in the field among the older denominations, or we must make one
of our own. Independency is exposed to too many dangers.

Some of the "difficulties" in such a union, McClurkan observes,
included the length of the denominational name, how the program
of twenty-eight missionaries would be cared for, a broad base of doctrinal agreement that went beyond the extremes of Calvinism and
Arminianism, strengthening the holiness movement by more emphasis on grace and the keeping power of God, and better teaching on
what follows sanctification, including clarification of the distinction
between humanity and sin. McClurkan concludes, "We believe that
holiness churches started during the last 28 years are too narrow…
they lack in both depth of teaching and breadth of thought. We want
something that embraces all the essential features of the holiness
Church plus every advantage that comes to us from wider outlooks."

Bresee's reply to McClurkan is dated August 1, 1907, and says
that the doctrinal basis of belief should be "very simple and embrace
what is essential to holiness." Nonessentials should be relegated to
"personal liberty," by which he meant that "a person has a right to
hold a belief and to recognize the same right in another to believe
differently without fussing about it." Bresee explained, "We hold that
any truth about which there can be two theories, and a person can be
holy and believe either theory… should be relegated to individual liberty. All can agree on holiness… and agree that every one shall think
for himself and not for others on things not essential to holiness."
Bresee understood this distinction between essentials and nonessentials as the gist of what McClurkan had said, and it was the platform
of the Nazarenes. Bresee concludes, "This must be the ground of
union: in the great essentials, unity; in nonessentials, liberty."

These letters were exchanged just prior to the gathering of the
Church of the Nazarene in the West and the Association of Pentecostal
Churches of America in the East to form the Pentecostal Church of
the Nazarene in Chicago in October 1907. The Nazarenes had invited
the Pentecostal Mission to send fraternal delegates to this Chicago

Assembly, and Brother McClurkan was asked to appoint a committee to attend.[157] The "Minutes" of the Pentecostal Mission give no names of those who attended nor any report of the meeting. Timothy Smith says, "A strong delegation from the Pentecostal Mission attended the Chicago assembly. They received a hearty welcome, and prospects for their union with the new movement at Pilot Point, Texas, the next year seemed bright."[158]

The Pentecostal Mission was invited to send representatives to the General Assembly of the Pentecostal Church of the Nazarene to be held at Pilot Point, Texas, in October of 1908, at which time the Holiness Church of Christ in the Southwest joined with the Nazarenes.[159] The following were elected by the Eleventh Annual Convention on October 2, 1908, to represent the Pentecostal Mission: J. O. McClurkan, A. S. Ransom, John T. Benson, E. W. Thompson, D. E. Scott, S. W. McGowan, and Tim H. Moore.[160] The group was instructed to "confer with the Nazarene brethren relative to a union and report to the Convention to be called for that purpose." On the long trip by train, "there was considerable discussion over the *Manual* of the Pentecostal Church of the Nazarene, with such changes marked as [the group] desired."[161] The Mission brethren were well received and were invited to sit in with the *Manual* Revision Committee. They "found a body of earnest, devout people with their hearts very set on the propagation of the gospel of our Lord and Savior, Jesus Christ."[162] Upon their return, the Committee made the following recommendations to the Special Convention, recommendations which were unanimously adopted:

1. We find that they [Nazarenes] are not sufficiently committed to the doctrine of the Lord's pre-millennial Second Coming to justify us in organic union as yet.

2. We seriously question the scripturalness of ordaining women as elders as their custom is.

   With regard to the other points involved in their doctrine and polity, we think that in common council they could be amicably adjusted. However, we do not deem it advisable to cease our negotiations with these excellent people, but recommend that negotiations be continued… that a Commission be appointed… to confer with them… on the two points involved….[163]

"No two subjects could have been found upon which the Nazarenes would have been less willing to compromise," observes Timothy L. Smith.[164] Premillennialism ran counter to the views of both Bresee and Reynolds, general superintendents in the Pentecostal Church of the Nazarene, as well as to the views of many others of Methodist background who held to a postmillennial belief. It is likely that Bresee anticipated this objection when he replied to McClurkan's letter in 1907, a letter that was mentioned earlier: "We hold that any truth about which there can be two theories and a person can be holy and believe either theory… should be relegated to individual liberty." Moreover, on the ordination of women, every parent body from which the Nazarenes had come owed much of its success to the work of dedicated women in the pulpit, and all had adopted provisions for the ordination of women.

Surely there were "deeper issues" involved besides premillennialism and the ordination of women as to why McClurkan and his Mission could not bring themselves to join the Nazarenes. John T. Benson Jr. in his excellent work entitled *A History of the Pentecostal Mission, 1898–1915* suggests several additional reasons: (1) jeopardy of the Pentecostal Mission Foreign Missionary Program, which he sees as the over-riding reason, (2) pervasive influence of the Eleventh Hour Movement which left no time for denomination-building, (3) a lurking distaste for denominationalism and ecclesiasticism.[165]

At the Annual Convention of 1909, the union question was considered again. The Special Committee on "Organization or Affiliation with Other Bodies" gave this report: "The Pentecostal Mission has reached a crisis in its existence where its unorganized system fails to satisfy its people and to promulgate its doctrine. It seems to us there are two courses open: 1. The affiliation with another body; 2. To organize within ourselves and definitely push the work in our own field. We recommend the carrying out of the latter."[166]

The second suggestion in this report—to better organize among themselves—was adopted, and the following committee was elected to draw up further recommendations: J. J. Rye, S. W. McGowan, and

John T. Benson. After a study of the by-laws and rules governing the Pentecostal Mission, it was reported that ample provision existed for the organizing of churches, bands and missions, with arrangements for pastors, a field secretary, and districts, and for proper representation of local congregations in the Annual Conventions. However, such a plan to organize their own work more thoroughly was voted down after lengthy discussion.[167] Then a suggestion by McClurkan to continue the present plan until the next Annual Convention was accepted, at which time the church question should be settled in one of three ways: (1) either by being allied to some kindred organization, (2) or by forming one of their own, (3) or by withdrawing entirely the Pentecostal Mission from the oversight of the congregation with the recommendation that this feature of the work be left to regular church organizations (other denominations).[168]

Benson states that "pressures were upon [McClurkan] to either organize or unite with another denomination. His people were restive. There were danger signals of a possible division and lack of unity."[169] The third alternative, "to let other 'regular church organizations do the organizing,'" may have been more representative of McClurkan's thought and feelings as things developed over the next few years. "He would not oppose any who wanted to join or become a part of a denomination," says Benson, but "his mission was Bible training in the classroom, [pastoring] the Pentecostal Tabernacle, [editing] the *Living Water* weekly paper, and [sending] missionaries to Foreign Fields."[170]

The year 1910 was a crucial time for McClurkan and the Pentecostal Mission as they continued to struggle with the issue of joining the Church of the Nazarene or of organizing into churches themselves. At a called meeting of the General Committee of the Pentecostal Mission on June 24, 1910, John T. Benson made a motion to invite the Nazarene Committee to come to Nashville to meet with the Mission Committee as soon as possible. The motion passed. The "Minutes" of the Executive Committee's next meeting (September 28, 1910, the last meeting prior to the opening of the Thirteenth Annual Convention) state that Benson moved that the "Nazarene brethren be invited here next week." The motion passed unanimously. The Nazarene delegation consisting of General Superintendents Bresee, Reynolds, and

Ellyson, along with evangelist Bud Robinson, a Tennessean by birth, arrived and met with McClurkan's group on October 3 and 4, 1910. After a brief historical sketch of the Pentecostal Church of the Nazarene by Dr. Bresee and one of the Pentecostal Mission by Brother McClurkan, McClurkan then discussed the points desired by the Mission. Bresee replied that the missionary headquarters could be located in Nashville, that a statement against lodges and tobacco could be arranged, that the name of the Pentecostal Church of the Nazarene was too long but that he hoped the word "Nazarene" would be kept in it, that he did not think that the statement on the ordination of women could be changed, that the statement on the coming of the Lord was a hard one and that he believed a man could be either a premillennialist or a postmillennialist and be a holy man, that veto power was not lodged in the general superintendents but in the General Assembly, that the statement of "all sin" instead of "inbred sin" was satisfactory, and that he would be glad to find a way of collecting funds for missions better than their own. There was "free discussion by Brother McClurkan and Dr. Bresee on all the points at issue… without any agreement."[171] The meeting ended at 6:30 p.m., and the participants agreed to meet again the next day.

The Convention met the next morning at 8:30 to hear a progress report on the negotiations of the previous day by the two commissions. McClurkan stated the need for prayer and his belief that the Lord would guide them, but he declined to say whether he would unite with the Pentecostal Church of the Nazarene. The "Minutes" record that there were "many motions and discussion, but none of which were satisfactory to Brother McClurkan."[172] And then the secretary records a rather strange turn of events: Brother McClurkan excused himself to go and teach a Bible class, and Brother Benson was called to chair the meeting. While McClurkan was absent, Tim Moore made a motion that, if they could get what they wanted on doctrinal points, they would unite with the Nazarenes. Brother J. J. Rye seconded the motion, and after much discussion the motion passed with thirty-four voting to join the Nazarenes and three abstaining. Chairman Benson "appointed himself a committee of one to inform Brother McClurkan" of the Convention's action, after which a recess was called until 1:30 p.m.[173]

John T. Benson Jr. provides an interesting commentary about his father's action: "Oh! My good Father! John T. Benson! The drama and circumstances of it all bring a lump in my throat and tears to my eyes. Think of it! He had been in the chair vacated by J. O. McClurkan and presided while the Convention voted to unite with the Nazarenes. It is as if the brothers and sisters had voted against the beloved McClurkan…. What was to be said to his friend and leader, J. O. McClurkan, who had led him into the experience of 'sanctification'?"[174]

At 1:30 p.m. the Convention reconvened with McClurkan in the chair. Brother McClurkan "again" stated his position and declined to say whether he would go with the Pentecostal Church of the Nazarene. The "Minutes" record that "several speeches were made regarding same. Nothing done."[175]

At 4:00 p.m. on October 4, 1910, the Mission Convention was asked to remain in prayer while the Nazarene Commission and Mission Commission met in private session. After prayer by Dr. Bresee, McClurkan made a "free, frank statement as to his difficulties on the doctrinal points, many questions being asked by Dr. Bressee. They [the Nazarene brethren] then agreed to take Brother McClurkan into free fellowship and love and confidence and that he shall have freedom of the Spirit in his teachings, which cleared the way very much for Brother McClurkan."[176] But when the Articles of Agreement for the basis of union were presented by Brother Bresee, Brother Benson would not vote for them (was he protecting McClurkan from the embarrassment of saying "no" to Dr. Bresee?), and then, secretary Tim H. Moore records that Brother Bresee proceeded "to give us a pretty sharp lecture as to our actions and which no doubt was sufficiently warranted to some extent."[177] After the Nazarene delegation had left, the Convention reversed its previous decision, and voted twenty-one to five against joining the Church of the Nazarene and nineteen to three in favor of organizing among themselves.

It seems that Dr. Bresee had made every concession possible to McClurkan, and although it appears that most of the Mission people would have preferred to unite with the Nazarenes, out of respect for their leader they would not go against him. Nevertheless, McClurkan and the Pentecostal Mission kept the door open by inviting the Nazarenes to come to Nashville for their Third General Assembly in

1911.[178] While it might seem that this invitation implied that the Mission might be ready to join the Nazarenes at that time, upon further consideration the invitation was altered in a letter McClurkan wrote to General Superintendent Ellyson a week later which removed any obligation on either side. Timothy Smith[179] reports that letter: "After our meeting adjourned and we had time to quietly consider the matter further, it occurred to us that perhaps it would be better for you to come to Nashville without any official recognition of us at all; just meet here like you would in any other city. We would provide for your entertainment and look after all matters of that kind,… and let you in no sense be obligated to us. You remarked in our first meeting last summer that you would not again go to a place on trial, and perhaps this is wise." Smith adds that "if the Lord desired to bring the two churches together perhaps it could be done more efficiently if both were left 'absolutely free for the present'.… If the assembly did meet in Nashville and the Pentecostal Mission did not unite with the Nazarenes, [McClurkan] added, 'the brethren wanting the organization would unite with you anyway.'"

The Board of General Superintendents was reluctant to accept the invitation knowing that McClurkan and the Pentecostal Mission would probably not unite with them at that time. Ellyson was not in favor of meeting in Nashville unless the Mission people would come in with the Nazarenes. Neither was Bresee inclined to take the Assembly to Tennessee under such circumstances. When it seemed that there might be a decision to go elsewhere for the Assembly, the Executive Committee of the Pentecostal Mission invited H. F. Reynolds to come to Nashville "at once" for further planning.[180] After extended negotiations, Reynolds came to Middle Tennessee and, with McClurkan's blessing, organized the Clarksville District of the Pentecostal Church of the Nazarene in the spring of 1911, the first organizational stake for the Nazarenes in Middle Tennessee. Reynolds appointed J. J. Rye, a Cumberland Presbyterian and longtime supporter of McClurkan, as district superintendent. "One cannot help but see McClurkan's own hand in this move," says Wynkoop. "It said silently to all concerned, 'I can't go into the Nazarene Church, but I want you, my children, to get in.'"[181] Reynolds and Ellyson then decided to take the General Assembly to Nashville, despite Bresee's reluctance and despite there

The 1911 General Assembly of the Pentecostal Church of the Nazarene held in Nashville, Tennessee

being no promise of union by the McClurkan group.[182]

The Third General Assembly of the Pentecostal Church of the Nazarene met in Nashville October 5-14, 1911. One day earlier, the Fourteenth Annual Convention of the Pentecostal Mission convened at the Nashville Tabernacle. According to John T. Benson Jr., the plan was to hold the Convention at the same time as the General Assembly, with the Convention meeting in the smaller auditorium on the third floor and the Assembly meeting in the larger auditorium on the street level. As it worked out, the Mission transacted all of its business in two days, the day prior to the Nazarene General Assembly and the last day of the Assembly.[183] This schedule enabled McClurkan and his Mission group to attend virtually all of the Nazarene Assembly.

The Nazarenes conducted ten days of business, inspiration, and preaching in the Pentecostal Tabernacle, with the larger evening and Sunday services held in the Ryman Auditorium at the back of the Tabernacle. General Superintendents Bresee and

Reynolds presided (Ellyson was not present). Three significant decisions were made by the 1911 Nazarene General Assembly that related to the Pentecostal Mission. First, Edward F. Walker was elected general superintendent to replace E. P. Ellyson, who had accepted the presidency of the college at Pasadena, California. Walker, a former Methodist minister and Presbyterian holiness evangelist well known by McClurkan and the Mission people, had joined the Pentecostal Church of the Nazarene in 1908. Asked to preach on the first Sunday of the Assembly, he swept the congregation off their feet with his eloquence and powerful delivery and on Thursday was elected general superintendent.

Second, B. F. Haynes was elected as the first editor of the new, official Nazarene paper, *Herald of Holiness*. Haynes, a former Southern Methodist holiness pastor, had been editor of *Zion's Outlook* before McClurkan's group took it over in 1900. He joined forces with McClurkan in the Pentecostal Alliance in 1898 and was one of the original seven members of the committee selected to oversee the Alliance. After serving as president of Martin College in Tennessee and Asbury College in Kentucky, Haynes became dean of the department of theology of Texas Holiness University under A. M. Hills and soon united with the Nazarenes.

Third, the Assembly approved two new additions to the General Rules: a rule against the use of tobacco and a rule against secret societies or lodge membership, additions which McClurkan strongly advocated. Nevertheless, the Assembly adjourned with union still unattained.

Meanwhile, the Pentecostal Convention met in session one day before the General Assembly on October 4, 1911, and the "Minutes" record that "Brother McClurkan called the Convention to order and stated that the Pentecostal Church of the Nazarene was here to hold their General Assembly and that our consolidating with them was up for consideration." Several speeches were made regarding the advisability of uniting with the Nazarenes, and a committee was appointed to confer with the Nazarene leaders. The committee reported back to the Convention on October 14 that "it is the sense of this Convention that the time has come when the organized work of the Pentecostal Mission should identify with the Pentecostal Church of the Nazarene."[184]

Then the "Minutes" record the following actions that took place after further negotiations: (1) The Pentecostal Mission was expected to take care financially of its missionaries for one or two years. (2) It was agreed that, should the Nashville congregation go with the Nazarenes, Brother McClurkan could remain as pastor if he would agree to join the Pentecostal Church of the Nazarene. Action was postponed for a few days.[185] There is no record that these issues were addressed in a few days or a few weeks.

Here again union with the Nazarenes was so close but not quite a reality. "Devotion to their leader… triumphed over the practical concern the laymen of the Mission felt for the increasing financial difficulties facing their home and foreign work," observes historian Timothy Smith.[186] It became obvious by this time that McClurkan would not join the Church of the Nazarene. A possible reason for his decision may be learned from McClurkan's editorial in the *Living Water* issue dated October 5, 1911, the opening day of the Nazarene General Assembly in Nashville. M. E. Redford analyzes that editorial:

> Mr. McClurkan discussed the Nazarene Movement. While on the one hand, he praised the work it was doing, on the other hand, he stated his firm conviction in the value of undenominational work. He believed in some organization, but feared that it might, if carried much farther, become a hindrance to the work of the Lord. He said that there was far too much denominational zeal and not enough of the Spirit of Christ. He had no desire for building up an "ism." He said to his people, "Brethren, beware of being churchly. Hold to lofty ideals. Keep your standards piercing the heavens. Do not set yourselves to build up another ism on earth, but exalt Christ. Establish centers for evangelical fervor. Tarry much in the divine presence. Avoid grafting on the doctrinal stump of any particular sect. Choose the best you can find among all the people of God. Welcome to your midst the poor and good of all lands. Take care of the poor. Preach the gospel in prisons, asylums, on street corners, in the homes of the lowly, in tents, under brush arbors, in sheds, on camp grounds, in school houses, plain churches, great cathedrals, in fact, everywhere you have any opportunity. Walk humbly and softly before the Lord. Keep filled with the Spirit, and like the Master go about doing

good and then there will be a place and a good place for you among the sisterhood of denominations."[187]

Merle McClurkan Heath was convinced that this bias against denominationalism was her father's basic reason for not joining with the Nazarenes. She affirms that McClurkan felt called to "undenominational work" and that "he saw the experience of sanctification as a truth too big to be confined within any one denomination," but was something all denominations should share."[188] Wynkoop asserts that the concessions made by the Pentecostal Mission and the Pentecostal Church of the Nazarene in 1911 left the Nazarenes with the perception that "the land is ours for the taking."[189] "A year later," she says, "Dr. Bresee, J. O. McClurkan, and Mrs. McClurkan also preached in a great open-air revival meeting in Erin, Tennessee. The pieces were falling into place."[190]

The Fifteenth Annual Convention of the Pentecostal Mission which convened on October 25, 1912, thought that it should continue its work on a nondenominational basis unless the Lord led otherwise. A committee was appointed to "take under advisement, and report to the next called or regular Convention, any suggestions or recommendations that they would think would add to the effectiveness of the present method of work."[191]

One of the outstanding features of the Pentecostal Mission was its intense missionary spirit. There was a feeling of divine responsibility to give the full gospel to the whole world. In the "Minutes" of the Pentecostal Mission for November 15, 1912, and May 5, 1913, the emphasis was on foreign missions. "It is plain to see that the bent and drive of Brother McClurkan was for Foreign Missions and not for organizing churches in the homeland," states Benson. "He had considered the organizing of churches, always to pull back, believing himself to be an Eleventh Hour Laborer in the vineyard of the Lord.... Never again would he consider the possibility of setting aside Education and Foreign Missions for the organizing of churches at home."[192] McClurkan's last Pentecostal Mission Convention to preside over and attend convened in the Nashville Tabernacle on October 3, 1913. There were no pressures to "organize or unite," and foreign missions continued to be McClurkan's major concern. [193]

J. O. McClurkan's last few months were filled with the work of the Pentecostal Mission and Trevecca College, work which included promoting home and foreign missions, overseeing publishing interests, editing the *Living Water* weekly paper, regularly preaching the weekly services of the Tabernacle, developing Trevecca Hospital and a "rescue home" known as Door of Hope for unfortunate girls along with the Pentecostal Training Home for Girls (orphanage), serving as president of Trevecca College and teaching his beloved students, and working on details of Trevecca's move to a new location for the fall of 1914. The burdens were too heavy for one man to bear, and McClurkan became seriously ill with typhoid fever.

As McClurkan lay near death in Nashville in September 1914, he talked to his wife about the event he knew was near. "Papa, what will we do about the Mission?" Mrs. McClurkan asked. "His answer was that they should unite with the Nazarenes."[194] Within a few days on September 16, 1914, on the day school was to open on the new campus, J. O. McClurkan closed his God-crowned ministry on earth and went to his eternal reward at the young age of fifty-two. His death ended nearly forty years of service for the Lord, more than seventeen of which he lived in Nashville.

The funeral was held in the Pentecostal Tabernacle at 2:30 on the afternoon of September 17, 1914.[195] The auditorium was packed, and many were turned away. Dr. C. E. Hardy read the Scripture lessons from I Corinthians 15:12-26 and Revelation 21:1-7. He said, "I am reading these Scriptures because Brother McClurkan used them at every funeral I ever heard him conduct." The resurrection song, "Hallelujah! We Shall Rise," that McClurkan wanted sung at every funeral was sung.[196] Rev. J. J. Rye, one of McClurkan's closest friends, told how he was the first fruits of McClurkan's holiness preaching in Middle Tennessee. "I love him as I have never loved any other man. I have never come into contact with a human being who has ever been as great a help to me in my Christian life as this man." Dr. Hardy said, "I know of nothing more to say of Brother McClurkan greater than these two statements: He believed in God; and he loved humanity." Rev. John L. Brasher spoke: "I simply dropped a rose at his feet in sweet memory of my love for him and his love for me.... Though God takes His workmen, He carries on His work.... The greatest evidence of the greatness of his mind and heart is that the young people who sat day after day in his classes and heard him every Sunday and Thursday night, and were with him in his office, listened with greatest eagerness to all his utterances." Rev. Ira Landrith of Nashville said: "Unless I am mistaken, I am now looking into the still face of the first citizen of Nashville.... Who is the first citizen of any city? He is the man whose life helps most the largest number of other lives... who, like his Master, 'goes about doing good' to more people than anybody else has reached." Professor R. E. Smith of Ruskin Cave College gave this tribute: "J. O. McClurkan was our spiritual powerhouse. He supplied what is lacking in the modern pulpit—the touch of mysticism. What the Hebrews had as a nation, Brother McClurkan has as a man—the genius for spirituality." Finally, the *Nashville Banner* newspaper recorded what the civic leaders of Nashville thought of McClurkan:

> In the death of Rev. J. O. McClurkan, pastor of the Pentecostal Mission Tabernacle in this city, which occurred at a local infirmary this morning at 2:30 o'clock, there passed from Nashville one of its most beloved pastors and strongest forces in the upbuilding of local, moral, civic, and religious standards. Mr. McClurkan had been ill for forty-five days with typhoid fever.... The passing of Mr. McClurkan causes widespread sorrow, not only in Nashville but in many other places where both his work and his splendid personal characteristics were well known.... Mr. McClurkan had perhaps touched as many lives with a beneficial influence as any man in this city. No man or woman had fallen so low, according to the world's estimate, but that he was ready to hold out to them a helping hand.[197]

J. O. McClurkan was laid to rest in Mt. Olivet cemetery on Lebanon Road in Nashville, Tennessee. His tombstone is in the shape of a pulpit, symbolic of the centrality of preaching for McClurkan. On the pulpit is an open Bible carved in stone signifying the source of his preaching and ministry, and across the pulpit are the words "He lived for others." Wynkoop concludes, "Nothing could better express the dynamic of that man: Christian service. Simply and eloquently that tombstone epitomizes the burning heart of J. O. McClurkan."[198]

On Sunday, October 11, 1914, the Pentecostal Annual Convention held a memorial service for their deceased leader, Rev. J. O. McClurkan.

After several tributes had been made by those closely associated with Brother McClurkan concerning his life and work with the Pentecostal Mission, the following beautiful resolution was adopted:

> Whereas God in His love and wisdom has taken unto Himself our beloved pastor, who for more than eighteen years has walked before his people in the beauty of holiness, endeavoring always to lead them to a fuller knowledge of God;
>
> Whereas he has poured out his life, not only for his own flock, but for suffering humanity the world over;
>
> Whereas through faith, prevailing prayer, and indomitable energy he has erected monuments to the glory of God which are left to us as a sacred heritage;
>
> Resolved, that we his people will endeavor by the grace of God to walk in the way of Holiness and be true to the Heavenly vision;
>
> Resolved, that we too will render unto God acceptable services, looking unto Jesus the author and finisher of our faith;
>
> Resolved, that we, his people, extend to his bereaved wife and beloved children our deepest sympathy and earnest prayer that God will bind up their broken hearts.[199]

J. O. McClurkan's tombstone—"He lived for others"

Following McClurkan's death, the Mission and the College faced several pressing needs: (1) a pastor for the Pentecostal Tabernacle located at 125 Fourth Avenue North, (2) a president for Trevecca College now located on the Percy Warner estate on Gallatin Road in East Nashville, and (3) money to run both the Mission and the school, which might involve uniting with some church, the Nazarene Church being a live option.[200] In this emergency situation, the leadership mantle fell on the shoulders of two men, John T. Benson and C. E. Hardy.

Dr. C. E. Hardy succeeded J. O. McClurkan as pastor of the Pentecostal Tabernacle and as president of Trevecca College.

As early as October 10, 1914, Benson made the following motion, which was adopted by the Seventeenth Annual Convention of the Pentecostal Mission:

> That a Committee of five be appointed to ascertain the wishes of our people and should it be desired by the people to effect a union of the Pentecostal Mission with the Pentecostal Church of the Nazarene, provided suitable arrangements can be made, that this Committee have full power to make such a union and take such other steps as may be necessary to wind up the affairs of the Pentecostal Mission. Upon notice from this Committee, the proper officers are empowered to make such transfers as are necessary of property, both real and personal, to the Pentecostal Church of the Nazarene or others.[201]

For the first time a committee was given "power to act" without another Mission Convention to be held.

On November 14, 1914, Board Chairman John T. Benson called together the Pentecostal Tabernacle congregation to discuss the new problems confronting them, especially the calling of a pastor. This and other meetings finally resulted in the selection of Dr. C. E. Hardy as the new pastor of the Pentecostal Tabernacle in December 1914.[202]

Who would take charge of Trevecca College? J. O. McClurkan's wife and son, Emmett, ran the College for a year, with John T. Benson serving as chairman of the Board of Trustees and Emmett McClurkan as "temporary business manager." Then in July 1915, Dr. C. E. Hardy was elected president of Trevecca College.[203]

Both Benson and Hardy gave leadership in cementing the long-delayed union with the Pentecostal Church of the Nazarene, which would open up a wider financial base for both Mission and College. The union was finally consummated in Nashville on February 13, 1915, five months after McClurkan died. Representing the Pentecostal Church of the Nazarene were Dr. H. F. Reynolds, general superintendent; J. A. Chenault, Tennessee district superintendent; E. G. Anderson, general missionary treasurer; and R. B. Mitchum, member of the General Missionary Board and special representative. Representatives of the Pentecostal Mission included John T. Benson, C. E. Hardy, Tim H. Moore, and Edward W. Thompson. The Articles of Agreement which sealed the marriage on February 13, 1915, included the following provisions: (1) Leaders of the Mission were to declare themselves to be in hearty accord and sympathy with the Nazarene *Manual.* (2) The Missionary Program of the Pentecostal Mission would be taken over by the Nazarenes. (3) All ordained ministers and evangelists of the Mission holding certificates would be accepted by the Nazarenes. (4) All members of the Pentecostal Mission would become members of the Nazarene Church, unless they elected otherwise. (5) All Mission property would be turned over to the Pentecostal Church of the Nazarene. (6) *Living Water,* if continued as an independent paper, would open its columns to solicit money for the missionary program (*Living Water* continued as a publication until 1918).[204]

Dr. H. F. Reynolds gave a glowing report of this union with the Nazarenes in the March 19, 1915, issue of *Other Sheep,* missionary organ of the Nazarene Church. Reynolds estimated that the union bound together about 40,000 people who had the same work and that it brought into the fold fifty or more foreign missionaries.[205]

It should be noted that Trevecca College was not "adopted" when the parent Mission was united in marriage with the Pentecostal Church of the Nazarene in 1915. However, negotiations were soon started that resulted in the final adoption at the September 1917 Tennessee District Assembly held in Nashville. The report in the *Herald of Holiness* (October 31, 1917) was titled "Our Latest College" and said, "As an accredited school, the various courses are on a par with the best colleges of the land having preparatory departments as well as the regular collegiate courses carrying with them the attendant degrees."[206]

The beautiful tribute to McClurkan by Dr. Mildred Bangs Wynkoop is an appropriate conclusion to this chapter on McClurkan's life:

> J. O. McClurkan was a "good man." Goodness in McClurkan was coupled with strength and courage and vision, and he set in motion forces for good that transcended and over-shot the span of his brief life.
>
> … Goodness to McClurkan was no empty "Pollyannaism." It was the power of the "Terrible Meek" of Jesus. His eyes were on the needs of men around him. He spent himself in service— not clumsily, arrogantly, but with a tenderness, and empathy and grace that brought healing….
>
> A portrait of McClurkan would be a distortion without painting in his holy enthusiasm for missions. He believed with all his might that an apostolic missionary spirit is the result of the baptism with the Holy Spirit…. Many students called to missions trained in Trevecca. He said to them, "The Mission field is no dumping ground for failures," and proceeded to prevent failures by a strong course of training….
>
> True goodness has roots in the past and branches that spread wide and fruitfully over the tomorrows.
>
> As Trevecca reaches out toward the needs of the world today, attempting to bring the total relevance of the gospel to bear on the age-old problems of men in the new garb of need, she cannot outstrip the vision of the tall, lanky, Spirit-filled giant pacing out ahead of her. We, today, reap the reward of such a spirit…. Today, Trevecca stands… on tiptoe, reaching for the stature of its founder…

and looks again into J. O. McClurkan's clear- visioned eyes to find its own ministry laid out before it.[207]

<hr>

[1]John T. Benson Jr., *A History of the Pentecostal Mission, 1898-1915* (Nashville: Trevecca Press, 1977), 13; Timothy L. Smith, *Called unto Holiness* (Kansas City: Nazarene Publishing House, 1962), 180.

[2]*Zion's Outlook,* 11 April 1901, 1.

[3]Mildred Bangs Wynkoop, *The Trevecca Story* (Nashville: Trevecca Press, 1976), 41.

[4]Merle McClurkan Heath, *A Man Sent of God: The Life of J. O. McClurkan* (Kansas City: Beacon Hill Press, 1947), 12.

[5]*Zion's Outlook,* 11 April 1901, 1.

[6]Heath, 12-13.

[7]Ibid., 18.

[8]Ibid.

[9]Ibid.

[10]Ibid., 19.

[11]Smith, 181.

[12]The name of the college McClurkan attended in Texas was "Trinity College," not "Tucuna College," as was previously thought. This new information is based on a letter in the Trevecca Archives from Merle McClurkan Heath in which she refers to a letter from Walter McClurkan (J. O. McClurkan's first cousin) informing her that the name of the college was "Trinity College" in Tehuacana, Texas. Rev. Ira Landrith, one of the speakers at McClurkan's funeral, was a classmate of McClurkan at Trinity College.

[13]Heath, 24.

[14]*Zion's Outlook,* 11 April 1901, 1.

[15]Wynkoop, 42.

[16]Heath, 25.

[17]Wynkoop, 42.

[18]Heath, 27.

[19]Ibid., 28.

[20]Ibid.

[21]See Heath, 31-39, for a detailed description of her father's experience.

[22]S. W. Strickland, *A New Look at Rev. J .O. McClurkan* (Nashville: The Parthenon Press, 1960), 20. J. O. McClurkan's Bible was given to S. W. Strickland by the McClurkan family as an expression of warm and mutual friendship. Strickland presented McClurkan's Bible to Trevecca Nazarene College as part of the Founder's Day service on November 13, 1957.

[23]Trevecca *Darda* (1928), 10.

[24]Heath, 45.

[25]Wynkoop, 43-44.

[26]John T. Benson Jr. says that his father and mother, John T. and Eva Benson, found the experience of sanctification in one of McClurkan's tent meetings in the summer of 1897. John T. Benson, businessman and publisher, became a leading layman in the Pentecostal Mission. See Benson, 16-17.

[27]Benson, 20. Methodist "cowboy evangelist," Robert Lee Harris, conducted holiness revivals in West Tennessee in 1893 and "set in order" the New Testament Church of Christ in Milan, Tennessee, in July 1894. The New Testament Church of Christ merged with the Independent Holiness Church in Texas under the leadership of C. B. Jernigan in 1905 to form a new body, the

Holiness Church of Christ, which then united with the Pentecostal Church of the Nazarene in 1908 at Pilot Point, Texas.

[28]*Zion's Outlook,* 22 September 1898. B. F. Haynes, who later became the first editor of the Nazarene publication, *Herald of Holiness,* dates his own sanctification in 1894. Haynes edited the *Tennessee Methodist* and made it the holiness organ in the state until the Methodists withdrew their support in 1896, at which time Haynes changed the name to *Zion's Outlook.* When Haynes was financially unable to continue to publish *Zion's Outlook,* McClurkan's Pentecostal Alliance took over the publication in May 1900, with McClurkan as editor. In Erin, Tennessee, a "holiness house church" developed out of this revival in 1894, according to Rev. Robert S. Mitchell, long-time pastor of the Erin Church of the Nazarene, as told to him by four charter members of the Erin Church: Mr. and Mrs. Sid Boone, Mercer Bateman, and Dora Simpson. The Erin congregation became a part of the Pentecostal Church of the Nazarene in 1911. If this "house church" developed sometime between 1894 and 1896, it may be the oldest church in the South *in continuous existence* that became a part of the Church of the Nazarene.

[29]Heath, 53.

[30]Ibid., 55-56.

[31]Ibid., 56.

[32]Wynkoop, 46.

[33]Cited by Jasper White in his unpublished master's thesis (May 1973) for Indiana Central College, "A Man and a Mission: The Story of J. O. McClurkan and the Pentecostal Mission," 22.

[34]Benson, 21. This old church had been completed during the years of the Civil War, and in 1892 the Tulip Street congregation moved to the new location at the corner of Sixth and Russell Streets. This church was the one that John T. Benson Jr.'s father and mother attended, as well as his grandfather. See John T. Benson, *Historic East Nashville and Old Tulip Street Methodist Church* (Nashville: Trevecca Press, 1980). Subsequent endnote references to Benson all refer to his *A History of the Pentecostal Mission, 1898-1915.*

[35]Committee "Minutes," 14 May 1898.

[36]Wynkoop, 46. S. W. Strickland contends that the worship in the old Tulip Street Methodist Church marks the beginning of what later came to be called the First Church of the Nazarene. See Strickland, 32.

[37]Millard Reed, paper submitted to Professor Eugene Te Selle at Vanderbilt University, 20 December 1976, "A Brief Study of the Pentecostal Mission," 13.

[38]Benson, 21-23; Wynkoop, 46-48.

[39]White, 26.

[40]C. E. Hardy, *Trevecca Messenger,* December 1946.

[41]Strickland, 35-36.

[42]Wynkoop, 48.

[43]Emmett McClurkan, *Trevecca Messenger,* December 1945.

[44]Heath, 22.

[45]Benson, 23.

[46]Heath, 57.

[47]*Zion's Outlook,* 15 August 1901, 15.

[48]Benson, 23-24. There are no official records at the time of this First Convention. However, some time later, John T. Benson who was elected secretary of the Convention, "recorded the 'Minutes' from memory." Benson's son, John T. Benson Jr., feels that the fervency and fellowship of that First Convention were so overwhelming that keeping records seemed unimportant at the moment.

[49]"Minutes," First Annual Convention of the Pentecostal Alliance, 18-20 July 1898. See also M.E. Redford, "History of the Church of the Nazarene in Tennessee," B.D. thesis, Vanderbilt University, 1934, 34-35.

[50]Benson, 24. Dr. Millard Reed says of John T. Benson's assistance to McClurkan that "he is a guiding spirit from the 'second position.' …He obviously loves McClurkan as well as the work. He aids, serves, and sometimes guides and protects his leader. He maintains the necessary structures of organization that McClurkan had little inclination to engage in. While J. O. McClurkan is clearly the leader, his leadership would have been impossible without John T. Benson" (Reed, 7).

[51]Wynkoop, 32.

[52]Melvin Dieter, "The Development of Holiness Theology in Nineteenth Century America," *Wesleyan Theological Journal,* 20, No. 1 (Spring 1985), 66 ff.

[53]W.T. Purkiser, *Called unto Holiness* (Kansas City: Nazarene Publishing House, 1983), II, 24.

[54]See Benson, 93-95, for a discussion of the "tongues" issue in 1908 among McClurkan's group.

[55]Cited in Wynkoop, 50.

[56]*Zion's Outlook,* 22 September 1898, 2. The requirement for membership was changed at the Fourth Annual Convention in 1901 to include acceptance of the "statement of doctrinal beliefs." See "Minutes," Fourth Annual Convention, 30 October-4 November 1901.

[57]Ibid.

[58]Ibid.

[59]Benson, 25-26.

[60]Ibid., 25.

[61]For details of the Second Convention of 1899, see Wynkoop, 51-52; Benson, 27-28; Redford, 40; White, 37-38; and "Minutes," Second Annual Convention, 23-27 November 1899.

[62]Wynkoop, 52-54.

[63]*Nashville American,* 14 August 1900. Cited in Wynkoop, 55-56.

[64]Benson, 30. This old Hynes School building was the first grammar school building erected in Nashville, in 1862 during the Civil War. On Sunday the number of attendants was so large that arrangements were made to meet at the "Watkins Institute" for these large meetings. See Wynkoop, 57-59.

[65]Benson, 30-31; Wynkoop, 58-59.

[66]Wynkoop says that "the period between 1901 and 1915 can properly be classed as a unit because changes begun in 1901 led to events in 1915, particularly joining the Pentecostal Church of the Nazarene.... Several crucial decisions were made at the 1901 Annual Convention that set its course for the future" (59).

[67]"Minutes," Pentecostal Alliance Committee, 11 February 1901.

[68]Ibid., 1 August 1901.

[69]Benson, 38-41. John T. Benson later developed the Benson Printing Company and the John T. Benson Publishing Company.

[70]"Minutes," Fourth Annual Convention of the Pentecostal Alliance, 30 October–4 November 1901. J. O. McClurkan was elected chairman of the General Committee; J. H. Holmes was vice-chairman; Tim Moore was secretary; and John T. Benson was treasurer.

[71]In September 1901 the Executive Committee of the Pentecostal Alliance met at the Murfreesboro campground to confer with J. M. Pike of Atlanta regarding the question of organizing the holiness forces of the Southeast separately from the Christian and Missionary Alliance. See "Minutes," Executive Committee of the Pentecostal Alliance, 6 September 1901.

[72]"Minutes," Foreign Missions Executive Committee, 4 November 1901.

[73]Wynkoop, 61.

[74]*Zion's Outlook,* 7 November and 28 November 1901.

[75]"Minutes," Fourth Annual Convention, 30 October–4 November 1901.

[76]Ibid. Wynkoop states that "most of these affirmations were common to evangelical people, even holiness people, but two of them were interpretations not held as essential by the Holiness Association: 'verbal' inspiration, as distinguished from the basic fact of inspiration, and 'pre-millennialism' in contrast to 'post-millennialism' as most of the holiness leaders held. Also, the absence of reference to 'pre-venient' grace puts the form 'total depravity' solidly in the Calvinistic fold. These points are mentioned because they became matters of dialogue between Dr. Bresee and J. O. McClurkan regarding the union of the two groups. Both men desired a careful distinction between essential and non-essential beliefs for fellowship" (61).

[77]Ibid. See also *Zion's Outlook,* 7 November 1901.

[78]Wynkoop, 61.

[79]"Minutes," Fourth Annual Convention, 30 October-4 November 1901.

[80]Benson, 40.

[81]Ibid., 33. Benson says that his parents, John T. and Eva Green Benson, along with their three children, withdrew their attendance from the Tulip Street Methodist Church at this time and joined with McClurkan as attending members of the Pentecostal Alliance.

[82]Benson, 35. Wynkoop and Reed both cite Heath as saying these Bible classes led by McClurkan started in the winter evenings of 1899-1900. My reading of Heath that they began "the year previous" to the opening of the Bible Training School in November 1901 (65) would place the date a year later during the winter months of 1900-1901. Benson says these night Bible classes began in the early months of 1901 (35).

[83]Ibid., 40.

[84]Heath, 58.

[85]Edward Cox, "Tennessee Nazarene History," 3. A paper presented to the Tennessee District Church of the Nazarene Advisory Board on January 29, 1972.

[86]Heath, 62-63.

[87]Benson, 38. Wynkoop says that "as was true with John Wesley, J. O. McClurkan knew that the printed page was of more lasting value than preaching unless preaching could be augmented and supported by reading. So many of the converts were ignorant of spiritual things. McClurkan provided his people with inexpensive but quality pamphlets and small books as soon as he was able to produce them drawing material from a variety of sources" (52).

[88]Heath, 63.

[89]Benson, 56.

[90]Wynkoop, 60.

[91]"Minutes," Annual Convention of the Pentecostal Mission, 22 October 1904.

[92]The old Hynes building was exchanged for the new property at 125 Fourth Avenue North owned by one of the Pentecostal laymen, James H. Yeaman. The new property was purchased for $13,500 which included a payment of $6,500 for the old Hynes Building with the remaining $7,000 to be borrowed from Vanderbilt University at 6% interest. Additions to the new building to adequately house the Pentecostal Literary and Bible Training School cost another $2,000 which was provided by the three trustees: Tim Moore, John T. Benson, and Arthur Ransom. See "Minutes" of the Pentecostal Mission, 29 December 1904; 16 February 1905; 16 March 1905; Benson, 68-73; Wynkoop, 66; *Living Water*, 19 January 1905. For the significance of the Ryman Auditorium built in 1892 for religious and civic events, see Wynkoop, 69.

[93]"Minutes," Annual Convention of the Pentecostal Mission, 8 October 1905.

[94]"Minutes," Ninth Annual Convention, 4-8 October 1906.

[95]Benson, 80.

[96]"Minutes," Ninth Annual Convention, 4-8 October 1906. In addition, an application form was developed which asked for additional information from an applicant for a certificate. See Benson, 82.

[97]See the correspondence between McClurkan and Bresee at the end of Chapter III in this book.

[98]"Minutes," Ninth Annual Convention, 4-8 October 1906.

[99]Ibid.

[100]"Minutes," Tenth Annual Convention of the Pentecostal Mission, 3-7 October 1907.

[101]Cited by Wynkoop, 62.

[102]Benson, 35; Wynkoop, 62; Heath, 65; Eugene Williams, "History of Trevecca Nazarene College," B.D. thesis, Nazarene Theological Seminary, 1956, 19-20.

[103]Cited by White (90) and based on a personal interview with Merle McClurkan Heath, 15 June 1972.

[104]Williams, 18.

[105]Wynkoop, 62.

[106]*Zion's Outlook*, 7 March 1901.

[107]Wynkoop, 64.

[108]J. O. McClurkan, "Bible Training School," *Zion's Outlook*, 30 May 1901, 8. A distinctive characteristic of the new school was to be the combination of "academic training" with "practical

training." For the practical side, see Benson, 55-56.

[109]Wynkoop, 64.

[110]Ibid.

[111]Ibid. The "Minutes" of the Pentecostal Alliance, 25 September 1901, show W.M. Tidwell to be admitted to membership in the Alliance and given a certificate as a lay evangelist. As one of Trevecca's first graduates, Tidwell was sent by McClurkan to begin work in Chattanooga in 1903, where he established a growing mission which eventually became First Church of the Nazarene in Chattanooga. Tidwell Hall on the campus of Trevecca Nazarene University was named in honor of its first student. See J.E. Cook, *W. M. Tidwell (A Life That Counted): The Life of William Moses Tidwell* (Ann Arbor, Michigan: Malloy Lithographing, Inc., n.d.)

[112]Heath, 65-66.

[113]Cited by Eugene Williams (23) and based on a personal interview with Mrs. McClurkan, 15 June 1955.

[114]Wynkoop, 65-66.

[115]Benson, 37.

[116]Wynkoop, 66.

[117]Ibid.

[118]Heath, 67.

[119]Wynkoop, 65.

[120]Ibid.

[121]*Living Water,* 19 January 1905, 8.

[122]Ibid., 14 September 1905.

[123]*Darda* (1951), 3.

[124]Wynkoop, 66.

[125]*Living Water,* 14 September 1905.

[126]Ibid., 19 January 1905.

[127]Ibid., 11 October 1906.

[128]Ibid., 24 June 1909.

[129]Wynkoop, 79; Strickland, 75-76.

[130]Strickland, 80-82. Trevecka is both the name of the home of Rebecca Prosser and the nearby small village. Nearly two hundred years after the death of Rebecca Prosser, Lady Huntingdon rented and renewed the old Trevecka Castle for her college.

[131]Based on research done by Professor William J. Strickland in a variety of dictionaries.

[132]Lucia Myers, "The Faith of Lady Huntingdon," *The New Christian Advocate,* December 1957.

[133]William M. Greathouse, "Trevecca College, A Vine of God's Planting," Founder's Day address at Trevecca Nazarene College, 14 November 1986, 3.

[134]Smith, 189.

[135]For the original Trevecka in Wales, see Strickland, 77-83; Wynkoop, 20-23, 81-82; *Brycheiniog,* Vol. XV (1971), edited by D. J. Davies, chapter on "Trevecka," by Gareth Davies, and chapter on "The Queen of the Methodists" (The Countess of Huntingdon) by Margaret Lane; Eifion Evans, *Howell Harris, Evangelist (1714-1773)* (Cardiff: University of Wales Press, 1974); Geoffrey F. Nuttall, *Howell Harris (1714-1773),* (Cardiff: University of Wales Press, 1965); M. Bickerstaff, *There Was a Man Sent… An Outline of the Story of Howell Harris of Trevecka and the Beginnings of the Calvinistic Methodist Church of Wales (Now Called the Presbyterian Church of Wales),* (Trevecka: Stephens and George, 1959). The Trevecka College started by Lady Huntingdon in 1768 was moved the year after her death in 1792 to Cheshunt near London, and the name was changed to Cheshunt College. In 1905 it moved again to Cambridge, England, where it is still in operation today as Cheshunt College fully aware of its roots in Trevecka, Wales. There is today another Trevecka College in Wales (College Trefeca) operating as the laity center for the Presbyterian Church of Wales (Calvinistic Methodism) founded in 1842 and tracing its roots back to Howell Harris.

[136]Greathouse, 3.

[137]Strickland, 83-84. It has been suggested that G. Campbell Morgan may have recommended the name "Trevecca" to McClurkan, but I can find no documentary evidence to support this view. Morgan did come to Nashville soon after the new name was adopted and spoke at McClurkan's Pentecostal Tabernacle (Strickland, 84). Morgan was also president of Cheshunt College, Cambridge (formerly Trevecka College), from 1911 to 1914 while he was minister at Westminster Chapel, London. He also made many visits to the United States and preached in many areas of the country but I can find no evidence of any contact with McClurkan prior to the visit mentioned above. See Jill Morgan, *A Man of the Word: Life of G. Campbell Morgan* (New York: F. H. Revell, 1951); and John Harris, *G. Campbell Morgan: The Man and His Ministry* (New York: Fleming H. Revell Company, 1930).

[138]Wynkoop, 79; Strickland, 76.

[139]Ibid., 80.

[140]Ibid., 81, 36.

[141]For the full text of the charter and a copy of the actual charter, see Wynkoop, 85, 261-262.

[142]Williams, 25.

[143]*Living Water,* 23 November 1911.

[144]Ibid., 12 February 1914.

[145]Ibid., 9 October 1913.

[146]*Nazarene Weekly,* 19 March 1972.

[147]Williams, 27-28. Based on a personal interview with Merle McClurkan Heath on 15 June 1955.

[148]Benson, 69-70. This Yeaman was the man from whom the Pentecostal Mission and Bible Training School purchased the Fourth Avenue property in 1905. In the Ninth Annual Convention of 1906, Mr. Yeaman introduced a resolution which would have made the Mission a denomination. The motion was tabled and eventually rejected. This rejection may have had a bearing on an estrangement developing between Yeaman and the Pentecostal Mission. See Benson, 69-70, 80; and Wynkoop, 73, 90.

[149]Strickland, 74-75; Wynkoop, 90; Williams, 34-36; White, 102-103.

[150]Wynkoop, 90.

[151]Smith, 190.

[152]*Zion's Outlook,* 22 August 1901, 8.

[153]In 1901, C. B. Jernigan led in the formation of the Independent Holiness Church in Van Alstyne, Texas, which later merged with the New Testament Church of Christ in 1905 to form the Holiness Church of Christ, which group then joined the Pentecostal Church of the Nazarene in 1908 at Pilot Point, Texas.

[154]Smith, 191.

[155]Wynkoop, 73.

[156]For the full text of the correspondence between McClurkan and Bresee in 1907, see Ch. 3 in this book entitled "Selections from the Writings of J.O. McClurkan."

[157]"Minutes," Tenth Annual Convention of the Pentecostal Mission, 3-7 October 1907.

[158]Smith, 194.

[159]The merger at Pilot Point, Texas, on October 13, 1908, between the Pentecostal Church of the Nazarene (representing East and West) and the Holiness Church of Christ (representing the South) is considered the official birth of the Nazarene denomination.

[160]"Minutes," Tenth Annual Convention of the Pentecostal Mission, 2 October 1908.

[161]Benson, 102.

[162]"Minutes," Special Called Convention of the Pentecostal Mission, 25 November 1908.

[163]Ibid.

[164]Smith, 194.

[165]Benson, 117-120. Wynkoop says that "the decision to unite with the Church of the Nazarene was an agonizing one not because there was any personal antagonism or even a serious doctrinal problem involved, but for reasons that touch much deeper issues—issues that were matters of conviction and emotion" (76). She goes on to mention several of these "deeper issues," including the

influence of the Eleventh Hour Movement, the American Holiness Movement which was concerned more with interdenominational fellowship, the financial problems of the Pentecostal Mission which a loosely organized fellowship could not handle, and the loss of autonomy and independence in which one is forced to submit to the structural "chains" which the Eleventh Hour Movement felt must be cast off in order to prepare for the coming of the Lord.

[166]"Minutes," Twelfth Annual Convention of the Pentecostal Mission, 1 October 1909.

[167]For the complete report that was voted down, see Benson, 125-126.

[168]Ibid., 126.

[169]Ibid., 127.

[170]Ibid.

[171]"Minutes," Pentecostal Mission, 3 October 1910.

[172]Ibid., 4 October 1910.

[173]Ibid.

[174]Benson, 136.

[175]"Minutes," Pentecostal Mission, 4 October 1910.

[176]Ibid.

[177]Ibid. For further details and commentary on the actions of the Mission Convention and Commission, see Benson, 134-142.

[178]The invitation came from the Executive Committee of the Pentecostal Mission in a meeting on November 22, 1910. Benson believes that the invitation suggests some "second thoughts" on the part of the Pentecostal Mission's "inner group" (McClurkan, Benson, Moore, and Thompson) and that the points of difference with the Nazarenes were not as unacceptable as they had once thought. He further maintains that Brother McClurkan's struggle within himself was not so much over the differences as it was centered in his deep commitment as an Eleventh Hour laborer (146).

[179]Smith, 196.

[180]"Minutes," Executive Committee of the Pentecostal Mission, 21 February 1911. It seems that McClurkan and the Mission brethren saw Dr. H. F. Reynolds as having a more sympathetic understanding of their situation (Benson, 146-147). Wynkoop states that the General Assembly probably would not have come to Nashville had it not been for the "very wise, perceptive, and ingenious leadership" of H. F. Reynolds (86).

[181]Wynkoop, 87.

[182]See letter written by Reynolds to Ellyson on March 15, 1911, in Nazarene Archives, Kansas City, quoted in White, 131, in which Reynolds urges Ellyson to support the idea of taking the 1911 Assembly to Nashville.

[183]Benson, 147-149. It is interesting to note that there were four religious conventions meeting in Nashville during this same week in October 1911. See the write-up in the *Nashville Tennessean and Nashville American*, "Four Religious Conventions to Be Held this Week," 6 October 1911.

[184]"Minutes," Fourteenth Annual Convention of the Pentecostal Mission, 14 October 1911.

[185]Ibid.

[186]Smith, 197.

[187]Redford, 79-80.

[188]Heath, 58-59.

[189]The information is taken from the 1912 assembly of the Clarksville District Pentecostal Church of the Nazarene, cited in Wynkoop, 87.

[190]Wynkoop, 87.

[191]"Minutes," Fifteenth Annual Convention of the Pentecostal Mission, 25 October 1912.

[192]Benson, 169.

[193]Ibid., 173-174.

[194]Smith, 198.

[195]Information about the funeral is taken from *Living Water*, 24 September 1914.

[196]For a copy of the resurrection song, see Benson, 180.

[197]*Living Water,* 24 September 1914.

[198]Wynkoop, 91.

[199]"Minutes," Seventeenth Annual Convention of the Pentecostal Mission, 11 October 1914.

[200]Wynkoop, 94.

[201]Benson, 177. The five members were John T. Benson, Tim Moore, C. E. Hardy, E.W. Thompson, and W. M. Tidwell.

[202]Wynkoop, 94-97.

[203]Ibid., 94-102.

[204]Complete texts of the Articles of Agreement of February 13, 1915, are found in Benson (192-194) and Wynkoop (259). It should be noted that in a letter dated February 2, 1915, W. M. Tidwell, a member of the committee from the Pentecostal Mission, recommends this union (Wynkoop, 259).

[205]Wynkoop, 100.

[206]Ibid., 102-104.

[207]Ibid., 13.

CHAPTER TWO

J. O. McClurkan's Theology

J. O. MCCLURKAN WOULD NO DOUBT DENY BEING A THEOLOGIAN, IF by that term one means a scholar who is trained in the technical aspects of the various doctrines of the Christian faith. He should best be characterized as a "folk theologian" in the same sense that Albert Outler used the term of John Wesley. Such "theological work" as he put in print focused almost exclusively on religious experience and evangelism, with one exception. That one exception had to do with eschatology, and this doctrine, too, certainly influenced his thinking about the importance of scholarly theological reflection as well as the practice of ministry. Perhaps the most dominant influence on his concept of ministry and education was an eschatologically oriented teaching known as the Eleventh Hour Movement. The nature of this movement was calculated to deny the importance of other than minimal training in the doctrines of salvation and Bible for the practice of evangelism since the end was at hand.

Most of McClurkan's writings drew heavily upon other persons' works, apparently very little being the result of his own creative efforts. He gave great emphasis to reports of the spiritual experiences of others, and evidently, like most of the holiness movement of which he was a part, much of his theological understanding was derived from these experiences as well as his own.[1]

An analysis of his writings and that of those persons who knew him well suggests that the one distinctive feature of McClurkan's theological contribution resulted from the fact that there was a confluence in his thinking of two streams of theology that arose in the religious awakening of the eighteenth century. One of these streams was Calvinistic and was associated with the names of George Whitefield and Howell Harris; the other was Arminian, the theological position of that aspect of the revival that revolved around John and Charles Wesley. The former came to him via his Cumberland Presbyterian background, and the latter was mediated to him by the American Holiness Movement with its significant modifications of pristine Wesleyan theology.

The original Trevecka College was established by Lady Huntingdon as a meeting place for dialogue between the followers of Whitefield and those of Wesley. While it cannot be unequivocally documented, it seems reasonable to suppose that McClurkan may have had this fact in mind when he appropriated that name for his own institution in Nashville, Tennessee.[2]

A statement published in 1906 regarding the "ecumenical" nature of Trevecca College seems to further support this identification: "The school is not committed to either the Calvinistic or Arminian system of theology, but is eclectic, choosing the best from each of these two great doctrinal movements. Pentecostal truth overleaps all denominational barriers and has its own system of teaching."[3]

This quotation incidentally suggests that McClurkan's understanding of the "Pentecostal" movement was somewhat different from that of the main body of the holiness movement and was not to be narrowly restricted to an emphasis on entire sanctification by the Baptism with the Holy Ghost as a second work of grace. A statement he made in *Zion's Outlook* also reflects this broader concern *vis-à-vis* the "second blessing": "We do not believe that the best results are obtained by confining ourselves chiefly to the second work of grace. Sanctification should be and must be the hub of the teaching, but the work will become narrow and superficial, unless other truths are taught in their relative importance. The holiness movement has suffered more from narrowness than from preaching a full gospel."[4]

An often-told story that appears in McClurkan's biography written by his daughter reflects this unusual balance of theological traditions. A young holiness evangelist by the name of J. B. Chapman, who later became a general superintendent in the Church of the Nazarene, was visiting McClurkan at the Bible Training School in Nashville, Tennessee. During their conversation, Chapman is reported to have said to McClurkan, "Some say you are a Calvinist. Is there any ground for such a report?" McClurkan quietly replied, "I work as though I might fall but rest as though I cannot fall."[5]

However, two of his writings deal with the subject of "entire sanctification." In *Wholly Sanctified*, which went through several editions, he basically reproduced the standardized formulations, scriptural apologetics, and applications of the American Holiness Movement as it came to expression in a series of books sometimes referred to as the "Great Holiness Classics." The introduction to this small book reflects a wise observation that the "theology" of Christian experience is not essentially related to the reality of experience. Hence, he was not dogmatic about the use of a certain nomenclature but was committed to the reality of a higher Christian life than nominal Christianity manifested and believed this higher life was the secret to the effectiveness of the Church in carrying out its mission in the world. It was insignificant to him what terminology was given to this higher life. His lack of dogmatism, no doubt, explains why he could circulate as models for his audience the spiritual biographies of persons from widely varying theological traditions, many outside the "holiness" movement.[6]

In the final edition of *Wholly Sanctified*,[7] McClurkan made some important modifications in the interpretations of "entire sanctification" found in the earlier editions and included them in an Appendix, under the title "Suggestions—A Deeper Death to Self." He identified several weaknesses in the prevailing folk theology of the holiness movement. His own writing in the body of the book reflected these same weaknesses, as he admitted in the Appendix. The major weakness, and one that continues to plague folk holiness theology, was no doubt the consequence of the polemical situation that prevailed in America during the years of the holiness revivals. The mainline Methodist Church had shied away from teaching sanctification as a second crisis experience in favor of "growth in holiness." In reaction, the "second blessing" people tended to make extravagant claims for what would occur in this moment of experience subsequent to conversion. Such claims resulted in a widespread feeling that "entire sanctification" was the *terminus* of the Christian life, but as McClurkan noted, experience invalidated many of these claims.

In an attempt to retain the decisive and definitive character of the "second blessing," McClurkan began to speak about a "deeper death to self" that led to the maturer levels of Christian experience. As he would say, these "deeper deaths to self" were necessary to the perfecting of the character. This emphasis created some tension with the mainstream teaching of the American Holiness Movement. But McClurkan realistically recognized that after this "second experience" there remained in many the uprising of motives, feelings and attitudes inconsistent with perfect love. These remaining manifestations would be addressed by this "deeper death."

In an attempt to deal with this issue, McClurkan introduced a distinction between the sinful self and a natural self. In the blessing of "entire sanctification" a person dies to the sinful self, but, he argued, there is a life-long dying to the natural self. While this distinction relies on a conceptuality of the self that could no longer be accepted as valid by contemporary theologians, his point is well taken. He is seeking to make the distinction that others made with the dubious distinction between purity and maturity. It is dubious because, properly understood in its original semantic meaning, "purity" admits of no increase; it is an all-or-none concept. But if we adapt the concept of "purity" to a volitional and ethical sense as did the Old Testament prophets (and as was delightfully expressed by Sören Kierkegaard in his classic phrase, "Purity of heart is to will one thing"), then McClurkan's insight is a massive step forward toward a proper understanding of sanctification that would be relevant to the contemporary situation.

This carefully nuanced distinction between "crisis" and "process" might be traced to the confluence of the two theological streams noted at the outset of this chapter. The Calvinistic branch of Methodism resulted in what came to be known as the Keswick Movement. Its distinctive feature was its emphasis upon the Baptism with the Holy Spirit which gave power to overcome the presence of inward sin. As popularly stated, Keswick taught the "suppression" of the carnal nature while the "Wesleyan" wing of the holiness movement taught its "eradication." The debate between these two interpretations became intense at times.

Like John Wesley himself, McClurkan recognized that this debate was essentially a semantic disagreement. If the nature of the Christian life were properly understood, the practical outcome of these two theologies was essentially the same. As he said in *Zion's Outlook*, "Much of the difference between them is simply a question of terminology and methods of stating truth."[8] If one notes carefully the names to which McClurkan looked as models, Keswick leaders would be peppered among them. One of the more prominent, and one that apparently was profoundly influential on McClurkan, was A. B. Simpson, founder of the Christian and Missionary Alliance. The Pentecostal Mission was for a time closely affiliated with this group.

On this point, Wynkoop makes a perceptive observation: "McClurkan was drawn to the Keswick Movement for its spiritual life and realistic appraisal of the weaknesses of human nature even in the Spirit-filled Christian but was well aware of the fact that major differences lay behind the many things held in common."[9]

Specifically, McClurkan was sensitive enough to the issues to recognize that the emphasis of the holiness movement on the "eradication" of inward sin was more biblical than the "suppression" emphasis, while at the same time being concerned for the practical consequences of an inadequate understanding of what this teaching meant.

Once again, while using the popular language of "folk theology," McClurkan made another very important distinction. He insisted that many of the problems of the holiness movement stemmed from seeking an "experience," an "it." This emphasis ultimately results in instability and "dryness," which he found to be widespread in the holiness movement. By contrast, McClurkan insisted that one should seek *the Giver*. This more personal distinction makes sense only in terms of a relational conceptuality. To establish a relationship with a person lays the groundwork for a life-long cultivation of that relationship that results in ethical consequences more and more appropriate to that relationship.

As with his other writings, McClurkan's literary contributions to the doctrine of last things basically reproduces the thought of others. In fact, in *Behold He Cometh*, he indicates the writers from whom he draws his material. All of them represent the formative leaders in the development of the teaching known as "Dispensationalism," and there is no apparent deviation from this position either in biblical interpretation, theological assumptions, or discussions of end-time events. In a word, McClurkan was a thoroughgoing premillennial dispensationalist.

Consistent with this view of the end, McClurkan was profoundly influenced by what was known as the "Eleventh Hour Movement." His views were apparently given shape by a book by Rev. F. L. Chappell to which he made extensive reference in both periodical and book. The concept was taken from Jesus' parable about the workers hired at various hours through the day until within one hour of the "end of the day," a final group was brought into the field to complete the harvest (Matt. 20:1-16). While the implications drawn from this parable by followers of the Eleventh Hour Movement have nothing to do with the purpose of the parable, they interpreted it to mean that the final consummation was at hand and that they were living in the "last hour" of this dispensation, thus the need for immediate action. This concept affected McClurkan's whole approach to evangelism, missions, and education.

Wynkoop's summary of the key features of this movement is excellent:

> This term ("Eleventh Hour") referred to an eschatological teaching that Christ's return was imminent, so near in fact that there was scarcely time to do more than preach, throw up cheap "sheds" in which to preach, and then to preach. Many young people could not wait for proper schooling and rushed out to evangelize so as to save as many "souls" as possible before the end. The specific emphasis of the Eleventh Hour Movement was a belief in the immediate premillennial return of Christ to set up his kingdom on earth for one thousand years. When this occurred the social ills of the world would be healed by Christ—a task then, that no Christian worker ought to spend precious time in attempting now. There was more urgent business at hand.[10]

This point of view was quite at variance with that of P. F. Bresee who insisted on adequate preparation, even in the face of a limited amount of time for service. No doubt it also influenced McClurkan's view of denominationalism and was perhaps one factor in his reluctance, and ultimate refusal, to bring his Mission into the Nazarene denomination. The preoccupation with the administration of a denomination would detract from the urgency of the mission to be carried out during this "eleventh hour."

Modern Wesleyan scholars may think that McClurkan's views on eschatology are not appropriate, but he did make some significant theological contributions to an understanding of the realities of the "sanctified life." His greatest relevance, however, was in his spirit, his compassion for the needy, his personal presence, and his vision for the work of world evangelization.

---

[1]Virtually every issue of *Zion's Outlook* (name changed to *Living Water* in 1903) had a spiritual biography on the first page, and it usually spilled over to the inner pages, usually the editorial page.

[2]This idea is the implication of S. W. Strickland's discussion (83).

[3]From *Living Water*, 26 July 1906, 12, quoted in Wynkoop, 77. While S. W. Strickland (76-77) claims that McClurkan was knowledgeable about the Wesleyan revival in England, it may be questioned whether he was aware of the theological nuances involved in the theology of Arminius. Actually, John Wesley himself did not have most of Arminius's works available to himself. Contrary to popular opinion, Arminius remained a Calvinist with only a few modifications (See Carl Bangs, *Arminius*). It is more than likely that in the context in which McClurkan worked, "Arminianism" was more or less equivalent to Pelagianism, and thus his balancing act was a sound theological move.

[4]*Zion's Outlook*, 28 February 1901, 8.

[5]Heath, Foreword.

[6]See his *Chosen Vessels*, for an example, or the regular presence of such in *Zion's Outlook*.

[7]Since the two editions available to this writer were not dated and since no other information could be discovered, I refer to what was obviously the later edition as the last, for reasons made clear in the text.

[8]*Zion's Outlook*, 30 May 1901, 8.

[9]Wynkoop, 32.

[10]Ibid., 33.

CHAPTER THREE

Selections from the Writings of J. O. McClurkan

Sanctification

THE CENTRAL ISSUE OF THE WESLEYAN MOVEMENT FOCUSED ON THE possiblility of "entire sanctification" in this life. As the Methodist Church more and more came to relax its emphasis on this point, the "second blessing" people came to offer extensive arguments for this possibility. Some of McClurkan's work reflects this widespread concern showing him to be at one with the holiness movement of the time. The following selections are taken from McClurkan's two books on sanctification: *Wholly Sanctified: What It Is and How It May Be Obtained* and *How to Keep Sanctified.*

1. ENTIRE SANCTIFICATION—A PRESENT POSSIBILITY

From *Wholly Sanctified*, Chapter 3, selected passages

1. Sanctification is obtainable because God commands it. "Be ye holy, for I the Lord your God am holy." "Follow peace with all men, and

holiness without which no man can see the Lord." "Be ye perfect, even as your Father who is in heaven is perfect."

To say that holiness cannot be acquired till death charges the Almighty with requiring an impossibility. Who dare bring such an accusation? If heart purity were an experience reached only through long years of sinning and repenting, our Father would not have required it *now*. That He commands present holiness leaves but the alternative of obtaining it or disobeying Him.

2. That sanctification is obtainable we insist, because it is promised upon certain conditions. "Then I will sprinkle clean water upon you, and you shall be clean; and from all your filthiness, and from your idols I will cleanse you." "Blessed are they that hunger and thirst after righteousness, for they shall be filled." "I will save you from all uncleanness." "The altar which sanctifieth the gift." "Whatsoever toucheth the altar shall be holy." Whosoever complieth with these conditions will be cleansed—sanctified. So saith the Word. He that denieth challenges the Divine veracity.

Reader, are you seeking holiness? If so, throw yourself on the promises of God, nothing doubting, and the blessing is yours.

3. Sanctification can be obtained because [it was] prayed for in behalf of the church by inspired men; yea, by our Savior Himself. "Now, the God of peace that brought again from the our Lord Jesus, that great Shepherd of the sheep through the blood of the everlasting covenant, make you perfect in every good work to do His will." "And the very God of peace sanctify you wholly; and I pray God your whole soul, and spirit, and body be preserved blameless unto the coming of our Lord Jesus Christ." "Sanctify them through thy truth."

These and many other passages are the prayers of inspired men for the sanctification of the church. The Holy Spirit would not inspire a prayer that could not be answered. God does not mock His people. These profound yearnings of the soul after purity can be satisfied now. What a solemn farce to pray for holiness, claiming at the same time that it cannot be obtained. Holy men of God knew that the sanctification of believers was His will, hence they prayed for it.

4. The doctrine of holiness is inculcated in Scripture exhortations. "Leaving the principles of the doctrine of Christ, let us go on unto perfection." "Let us cleanse ourselves from all filthiness of the

flesh, perfecting holiness in the fear of the Lord." Men, moved by the Holy Ghost, did not urge an impossibility. Present sanctification is your privilege. So they said.

5. The attainableness of sanctification is argued from the declaration of the Scriptures. "Jesus Christ is made unto us wisdom, sanctification and redemption." "This is the will of God, even your sanctification." "Our old man is crucified with Him that the body of sin might be destroyed." "For God hath not called us unto uncleanness, but unto holiness." These passages plainly declare sanctification to be the privilege and duty of all Christians. They are either true or false. If true, our doctrine is true; if not, the whole system is false. Let God be true though all others be contradicted.

6. The attainability of sanctification is contended for because it is professed to have been obtained in the Scriptures. "And such were some of you, but ye are washed, but ye are sanctified." "And that man was perfect and upright." "And they were both righteous before God, walking in the commandments and ordinances of God blameless." "Ye are witnesses, and God also, how holily and justly and unblamably we behaved ourselves among you that believed." Here we have a positive profession of the very grace we are teaching. "God is no respecter of persons." Holiness is not for only a favored few. All may pass beyond the veil, under the blood where pure love and joy prevail.

7. We argue for the doctrine from the fact that full provisions have been made for it. "Wherefore Jesus, also, that He might sanctify the people with His own blood, suffered without the gate." "For this cause was the Son of God manifested that He might destroy the works of the devil." "That He would grant unto us that we being delivered out of the hand of our enemies, might serve Him without fear in holiness and righteousness before Him all the days of our life." "And He gave some apostles, some prophets, and some evangelists and some pastors and teachers; for the perfecting of the saints, for the work of the ministry, for edifying of the body of Christ; till we all come in the unity of the faith and of the knowledge of the Son of God unto a perfect man, unto the measure of the fullness of the stature of Christ." The blood was shed outside of the gate, that His people might be sanctified. God is an economist. He provides for no impossibilities.

The fact that provisions are made for entire cleansing argues not only its possibility, but also its necessity. God is holy. He hates sin. He has a perfect cure for the dread disease. There is not a single text which allows continuance in sin, either actual or original. Sin is the same dark, hideous thing, whether found in angel, preacher, or devil. A perfect consecration to God and a perfect faith in the cleansing blood free from sin.

It is claimed by many that sanctification is not attained till death, but our Lord prayed for present sanctification, explicitly stating that He was not asking for their removal to heaven. "I pray not that thou shouldst take them out of the world, but that thou shouldst keep them from the evil"—John 17:15. "Sanctify them through Thy truth, Thy word is truth"—John 17:17. These disciples were Christians, but not wholly sanctified. Their motives were mixed with evil. Christ was not "crowned within." They were not perfect in love. In Gal. 4:19, the apostle prays for this perfecting grace in the heart of the young converts, "My little children, for whom I travail in birth again till Christ be formed in you." He had travailed for their conversion, and now travails again for their sanctification.

St. Paul was so burdened for the perfecting of the church that he likens his sufferings to that of a woman in childbirth. In Acts 20:32, the apostle specifies the means by which the church is sanctified. "And now, brethren, I commend you to God and to the word of His grace, which is able to build you up and give you an inheritance among them which are sanctified." In Acts 26:18, sanctification is said to be through faith. Rom. 1:11 mentions an establishing grace. "For I long to see you, that I may impart unto you some spiritual gift, to the end that you may be established." What grace is it that roots and grounds the soul in Christ? Rom. 5:1 speaks of the grace of justification, but the next verse reads as follows: "By whom, also, we have access by faith into this grace wherein we stand and rejoice in the hope and glory of God." Here is another grace received, like justification, through faith. This is the standing grace, and evidently the one he desired the Roman Church to have. Thank God there is a grace which cuts one squarely loose from the world, first by taking the world out of him, then by keeping him from its spirit. Sanctification is the only perfect cure for worldliness. For the literal meaning of the word sanctify is to take the world out of you. How much the world needs this keeping, standing grace. Year after year young converts are received into worldly churches only to add another layer to the stratification of backsliders. Standing grace is in demand in the shop, behind the counter, on the farm, in the Sunday School, at prayer meeting, and everywhere else. The medieval theology argument, that one cannot quit sinning, receives a death-blow in Rom. 6:11, "Likewise reckon ye also yourselves to be dead, indeed, unto sin." The twenty-second verse of the same chapter reads as follows: "But now being made free from sin, and become servants to God, ye have your fruit unto holiness and the end everlasting life." These passages mean just what they say. Quit sinning, was Paul's exhortation. 1 Cor. 3:1-4, shows, first, that regeneration did not free these babes in Christ from the carnal mind; second, that they could and should be freed from such a spirit.

For surely the apostle would not rebuke them for possessing what they could only be delivered from at death. They needed sanctification. 1 Cor. 7:1 is an exhortation to seek holiness and, if followed, frees from sinful habits. "This, also, we wish even your perfection"— 2 Cor. 13:9. In the eleventh verse they are commanded to be perfect. If Christian perfection is attained only at death, we are confronted by the queer spectacle of an apostle working, through the Holy Ghost, building up a church in a pagan city, getting them in a shape to do something, and then desiring the Lord to cut the whole work short by taking them to heaven. Such an interpretation would be palpably false and not entitled to a moment's consideration. In Gal. 2:20 we have an example of "Christ crowned within": "I am crucified with Christ, nevertheless, I live; yet not I, but Christ liveth in me; and the life which I now live in the flesh I live by the faith of the Son of God, who loved me and gave Himself for me." Here is the whole theory of holiness. Through a perfect consecration and faith you move out and Christ moves in to abide. He lives the life for you. It is not your holiness, but *His* wrought in and through you. It is not the dumping of a carload into your heart at once, but Jesus just dwelling in you and keeping you cleansed and free from sin, moment by moment, as the pebble in the brook is kept clean by the water constantly flowing over it.

Eph. 3:14-21 contains one of the most remarkable prayers ever written. "For this cause I bow my knees unto the Father of our Lord

Jesus Christ, of whom the whole family in heaven and earth is named, that He would grant you, according to the riches of His glory, to be strengthened with might by His spirit in the inner man; that Christ may dwell in your hearts by faith; that ye, being rooted and grounded in love, may be able to comprehend with all saints what is the breadth, and length, and depth, and height; and to know the love of Christ, which passeth knowledge, that ye might be filled with all the fullness of God. Now, unto Him that is able to do exceeding abundantly above all that we ask or think, according to the power that worketh in us, unto Him be glory in the church by Christ Jesus throughout all ages, world without end. Amen." If the soul is made strong according to God's ability to strengthen, if Jesus abides in the heart, if the entire life is rooted and grounded in love and filled with all the fullness of God, this is perfect love. Certainly, the apostle would not have prayed for this church to be sanctified had it not been possible. "Our Lord has a purifying grace for His church. Christ also loved the church and gave Himself for it; that He might sanctify and cleanse it by the washing of water by the word, that He might present it to Himself a glorious church, not having spot, or wrinkle, or any such thing; but that it should be holy and without blemish"—Eph. 5:25-27. It was said that He would purify the sons of Levi—the church. "Rejoice in the Lord always"—Phil. 4:1. Nothing less than the baptism of the Holy Spirit will enable one to do this. Sanctification puts an artesian flow of joy into the heart. "And the peace of God, which passeth all understanding, shall keep your minds and hearts through Christ Jesus"—Phil. 4:7. Justification gives peace with God, but here is a profound, deep, heavenly quietude mentioned, the peace of God, which, though it may be possessed in some degree before, is only enjoyed in its fullness after the heart has been entirely cleansed"—Col. 2:2. "That their hearts might be comforted, being knit together in love, and to all riches of the full assurance of understanding." St. Paul was praying that the church at Colosse might have that illumination of soul necessary to apprehend Christ in all His fullness. Christ is made unto us sanctification. Hence, to recognize Him as their sanctifier is included in the above prayer.

The church at Thessalonica had been organized about six months. They were not in a backslidden condition, for their work of faith, and labor of love, and patience of hope are highly commended. They were examples to all that believed in Macedonia and Achaia. Yet the apostle was praying night and day exceedingly, that he might see their face and perfect that which was lacking in their faith. They had faith for justification, they were wide-awake and aggressive, yet there was something lacking in their faith. What was that something? Was it not the apprehension of Christ in all of His fullness? He prayed that their hearts might be established unblamable in holiness before God. In 1 Thess. 4:3 He assured them that God desired their sanctification. Not only were they to quit sin, they were to shun the very appearance of it. "And the very God of peace sanctify you wholly; and I pray God your whole spirit and soul and body be preserved blameless unto the coming of our Lord Jesus Christ. Faithful is He that calleth you who also will do it"—1 Thess. 5:22, 23. Even so, grant it, Lord Jesus.

It is sometimes said that sanctification is the setting ourselves apart unto the Lord, but in 2 Thess. 2:13 sanctification is said to be a work wrought in us through the Holy Spirit. The oft-repeated argument that sanctification is only conversion or recovery from backsliding, receives its death knell here. This church was thoroughly converted, had not backslidden, and was growing in grace. Yet the great apostle prays mightily that they might be sanctified. See how this perfect love crops out in 1 Tim. 1:5—"Now the end of the commandment is charity out of a pure heart." This is equivalent to saying that love is the fulfilling of the law. A pure heart is freed from sin. Observe again how this thought crops out in 2 Tim. 2:21, 22—"If a man, therefore, purge himself from these, he shall be a vessel unto honor, sanctified, and meet for the Master's use, and prepared unto every good work. Flee, also, youthful lusts; but follow righteousness, faith, charity, peace, with them that call on the Lord out of a pure heart."

In Heb. 10:19-22 two distinct experiences are clearly taught. "Having, therefore, brethren, boldness to enter into the holiest by the blood of Jesus, by a new and living way, which He hath consecrated for us, through the veil, that is to say, His flesh; and having an high priest over the house of God; let us draw near with a true heart in full assurance of faith, having our hearts sprinkled from an evil conscience, and our bodies washed with pure water." These brethren were already Christians. They had entered the holy place—regeneration; but had not gone on into the Holy of Holies—sanctification. The holy place was entered through the blood; the Holy of Holies must be entered through the blood. They did not grow into the first experience; neither could they into the second. "The true heart" is the perfect consecration, "the full assurance of faith" is the perfect faith which precedes cleansing. These people, though regenerated, needed another grace; their hearts were not pure; they are exhorted to obtain sanctification. The veil, though rent, did not expose the Holy of Holies to the public gaze. It was still a hidden place. Sanctification is a hidden life. One passses within the veil, and it instantly closes behind him. This precious grace is not left lying carelessly about on the surface. It is a part of the deep things of God. None but the King's children desire it, and they must dig to get it.

We conclude this chapter by reference to 1 John 4:17, 18: "Herein is our love made perfect, that we may have boldness in the day of judgment; because as He is, so are ye in the world. There is no fear in love; but perfect love casteth out fear; because fear hath torment. He that feareth is not made perfect in love." While sinners there is no love for God, all is fear; most Christians live in a state where both love and fear exist. In sanctification all fear is banished, and, as pure love fills every part of the soul there is no room for sin. Such a soul is perfected in love. The cleansing blood has reached the remotest corners and deepest jungles of the spirit. God reigns within without a rival. The soul sings—

> "Now, rest, my long divided heart,
> Upon thy blissful center rest."

2. How to Live the Holy Life

The following selections illustrate McClurkan's practical concern for holy living and the realities of the sanctified life rather than theoretical formulations or exclusive focus on a moment of experience.

From *How to Keep Sanctified*, selected passages

The conflict is not over when you enter the sanctified life. The enemy within has been cast out, but sin in a thousand different forms lurks about you. To retain a pure heart requires the utmost vigilance. "Let him that thinketh he standeth take heed lest he fall."

The Israelites did most of their fighting after entering Canaan; but few conquests were made in the wilderness. It takes the grace of entire sanctification to guarantee continuous victory in a land of walled cities, giants, and thirty-one kings. You will have endless opposition, keener trials, and severer temptations in a life of holiness. But the gift of the Holy Spirit makes every man a soldier, and Christ in the heart causes him to be more than a conqueror. Storms may rage, men scoff, and devils howl, but hid in the pavilion of the Divine Presence you have perfect peace—Ps. 27:5.

You do the committing; he does the keeping. "I pray God your whole spirit and soul and body be preserved blameless. Faithful is he that calleth you, who also will do it"—1 Thess. 5:23, 24. "The Lord bless and keep thee"—Num. 6:24. "He will keep the feet of his saints"— 1 Sam. 2:9. "He shall give his angels charge over thee, to keep thee in all thy ways"—Ps. 91:11. "He that keepeth thee will not slumber"—Ps. 121:3. "Thou wilt keep him in perfect peace, whose mind is stayed on thee: because he trusteth in thee. Trust ye in the lord forever, for in the Lord Jehovah is everlasting strength"—Isa.26: 3, 4. "Holy Father, keep through thine own name those whom thou hast given me"—John 17:11. "Kept by the power of God through faith unto salvation"—1 Pet.1:5. "Sanctified by God the Father, and preserved in Jesus Christ,… that is able to guard you from stumbling, and save you before the presence of his glory without blemish"—Jude 1:24.

Temptation

Immediately after our Lord was baptized with the Holy Ghost he was led by the Spirit into the wilderness to be tempted by the devil— Matt. 3:1. Temptation is of divine appointment, hence there is no sin in being tempted. You sin only when you yield to the temptation. For instance, Satan may torture you with suggestions of evil thoughts, desires, or feelings. Failing to get you to endorse them, he will turn accuser, saying: "You are a pretty Christian. Ha, ha, ha! Professing sanctification! Why, you hypocrite, it is doubtful if a person having such thoughts as you have was ever justified." The devil has met many entering the threshold of a holy life and driven them back into the wilderness with just such accusations. First tempting you to sin, but failing at this point, he would persuade you that the temptation itself is a sin. Bear in mind that no thought, feeling, or desire which Satan may present to you can become yours until you *will* to have it so. As some old writer has quaintly said: "You can't keep the birds from flying over your head, but you can keep them from building nests there." You can't prevent the devil bringing his children and leaving them on your door-step, but you don't need to bring them in and adopt them as your own. Remember, the key to the situation is this: *Evil suggestions do not become yours until you put your endorsement on them.*

The holiest people are often the most fiercely assaulted by the devil. He shoots his biggest guns not at the babes in Christ but at those who are pressing on to know the fullness of God. It may be that as we advance in the kingdom of grace we have to grapple with a class of devils stronger than those we met in the beginning of our Christian life—some genius like a Napoleon or Caesar to intercept us on our march to glory. Paul tells us that we are to wrestle with wicked spirits in heavenly places. This much we know: the nearer we get to God the less we have of temptation on the physical side. Hence in the sanctified life the enemy approaches more under cover, in a subtle, abrupt, intricate, intense way. If he came, as sometimes fancied in childhood, with eyes like balls of fire, huge horns, teeth like those of a thrashing-machine, long tail, and the roar of a Numidian lion, then all would instantly flee from his presence. But instead he often comes as an angel of light in the person of some dear friend, some long-established habit, some cherished wish or desire. Then again he clothes himself in such reasonable, proper, and commendable attire that, if possible, he would deceive the very elect, yet the Spirit-filled man will be able to recognize and resist him. "For we are not ignorant of his devices"—2 Cor. 2:11.

The Lord Jesus was long and bitterly assailed by Satan, yet he sinned not. This is a guarantee that he will give you grace to do like-wise.

Temptations are a test of character. "Blessed is the man that endureth temptation; for when he is tried, he shall receive the crown of life"—Jas. 1:12. Yours are not peculiar; others have had similar testings. "There has no temptation taken you but such as is *common* to man: but God is faithful, who will not suffer you to be tempted above that ye are able; but will with the temptation also make a way to escape, that ye may be able to bear it"—1 Cor. 10:13.

Jesus knows how to sympathize with and deliver you. "For in that he himself hath suffered being tempted, he is able to succor them that are tempted"—Heb. 2:18. "For we have not a high priest which can not be touched with the feeling of our infirmities; but was in all things tempted like as we are, yet without sin"—Heb. 4:15. "For consider him that endured such contradiction of sinners against himself, lest ye be wearied and faint in your minds. Ye have not yet resisted unto blood, striving against sin"—Heb. 12:3, 4.

The Lord defeated Satan with the sword of the Spirit. He met every thrust with a quotation from the Scriptures—Matt. 4: 4-10. Ask him to do the same through you.

Feelings

Avoid laying too much stress on your feelings. Many have failed here. Not obtaining such an experience as they expected, they began to doubt, became discouraged, and dropped back into the old up-and-down life. Oftentimes seekers for heart purity become fascinated with some beautiful experience which they hear related, and will not be satisfied unless they obtain one just like it. This is a grave error. As there are no two people alike, so there will be no two experiences exactly the same. The Lord gives to each such as he needeth. Perhaps those who seek certain good feelings have the least of them. Fix the eye on Jesus, then the whole body will be full of light. The pleasurable and delightful emotions are the result of obeying God. Seek *him*, rather than *his gifts*. Having *him*, all his gifts are yours; While, on the other hand, you might enjoy many of his gifts without having him at all.

Madame Guyon said that the Lord sometimes withdrew all her joyous emotions, that she might be drawn closer to him. There is danger of making an idol of your experience, allowing the gift to come between you and the Giver. Sometimes we go home with our arms full of nice things for the children, and they become so absorbed in them that they neglect to climb up in papa's arms to lavish on him their accustomed tokens of filial devotion. Not much time to hug and kiss the giver while so many pretty things are on hand to be examined. Thus we may treat our Heavenly Father until he will withdraw the gift for a brief season that we may get our eye, faith, and love all centered on him again.

Rev. A. B. Simpson says that in seeking sanctification for quite a while he sought an "it." He would pray and pray until he had a certain good feeling. Then he would exclaim, "I have it!" when lo! It would fade as a morning cloud. Then the Lord showed him that it was not an "it" which he needed, but *himself.* Then he appropriated Christ as his Sanctifier, and the "its" or blessings followed. The difference between the justified and sanctified life is clearly set forth in the following hymn:

Christ Himself

Once it was the blessing, now it is the Lord;
Once it was the feeling, now it is his Word;
Once his gifts I wanted, now the Giver own;
Once I sought for healing, now himself alone.

Once 'twas painful trying, now 'tis perfect trust;
Once a half salvation, now the uttermost;
Once 'twas ceaseless holding, now he holds me fast;
Once the constant drifting, now my anchor's cast.

Once 'twas busy planning, now 'tis trustful prayer;
Once 'twas anxious caring, now he has the care;
Once 'twas what I wanted, now what Jesus says;
Once 'twas constant asking, now 'tis ceaseless praise.

Once it was my working, his it hence shall be;
Once I tried to use him, now he uses me;
Once the power I wanted, now the Mighty One;
Once to self I labored, now to him alone.

—A. B. Simpson

While a life of holiness is peculiarly noted for its joy, peace, and rest, there may be brief seasons, especially at its beginning, of heaviness through manifold temptations—1 Pet. 1:6. The devil may take advantage of ill health and bring about strange and unaccountable feelings of depression; but in the midst of these tunnels continue to rejoice in the Lord, for he abides just the same, and out of it all he will bring you into a sweeter and richer union with himself. Live only in him, and all will be well.

Consecration

You entered the sanctified life through consecration and faith. It is retained the same way. Remember that the gift must stay on the altar. You have irrevocably yielded all to God. Never take it back. It is so easy to compromise a little here and there—the world creeps in and Jesus goes out before you are aware of it.

Take an inventory once in a while to make sure that property, Church, family, plan of life, likes and dislikes, are all kept on the altar. This little verse expresses it all:

> I am willing
> > To receive what thou givest,
> > To lack what thou withholdest,
> > To relinquish what thou takest,
> > To be what thou requirest,
> > To do what thou commandest.

Should you find at any time that you have taken something off the altar, put it back instantly. Whatever he tells you to do, do it; don't try to dodge it, nor postpone it, nor excuse yourself from it, but do it at once. "Obedience is better than sacrifice." "Ye are my friends, if ye do whatsoever I command you"—John 15:14. "And he that keepeth his commandments dwelleth in him, and he in him"—1 John 3:24.

> O sacred union with the Perfect Mind!
> > Transcendent bliss, which thou alone canst give,
> How blest are they, this pearl of price who find,
> > And, dead to earth, have learned in thee to live.
>
> Thus in thine arms of love, O God, I lie,
> > Lost, and forever lost, to all but thee,
> My happy soul, since it hath learned to die,
> > Hath found new life in thine infinity.
>
> Oh, go and learn the lesson of the Cross,
> > And tread the way which saints and prophets trod,

> Who, counting life and self and all things loss,
>   Have found in inward death the life of God.
> —Prof. Upham
>
> Thou art the sea of love
>   Where all my pleasures roll;
> The circle where my passions move,
>   And center of my soul.

Faith

You have all on the altar for time and eternity. The Bible says that the altar sanctifies the gift—Matt. 23:19, that it maketh everything holy that toucheth it—Ex. 29:37. Christ is your altar. You have laid it all on him, and his blood cleanses you from all sin—1 John 1:7. When your faith appropriated these promises he sanctified you. Keep on believing them, and he will keep you free from sin.

There may be times when your feelings and the seemings say that you are not sanctified, but cling to—yea, rest on—the Word. The altar sanctifieth the gift: "I am the gift, therefore it sanctifieth me." Confess it over and over to yourself and to God, and the tempter will not tarry long. Cultivate the habit of trusting regardless of emotions. You doubt God just in proportion to what you require apart from the Word to make you believe it. To say that you are consecrated, and yet refuse to believe that he sanctifies you, simply challenges his veracity. The devil would delight in making you afraid to believe, but you had better be afraid not to believe.

The dear Savior says that if you keep his commandments he and the Father will come into your heart and make their abode there. Don't look in to see if he is there, and don't try to see him there, but *believe* that he is there because you are complying with the conditions on which he promises to dwell in you. He dwells in your heart by faith—Eph. 3:17. If you look to see if he is there, the *if* is the door through which he goes out.

Some one asked Mr. Müller the secret of his strong faith. He replied: "By standing firm amid severe testings." Abraham staggered not at the promises, and he became the father of the faithful. There would be more Abrahams if there were more who would stand such testings. "Faith is nothing apart from its object." It is hard to believe, looking at the difficulties; the longer you look the bigger they become. But when your eye and heart rest on Jesus, faith follows as a natural result. Peter did not begin to sink until he got his eye off Christ [and] on the waves. "Thou wilt keep him in perfect peace, whose mind is stayed on thee."

A friend of the writer so often closes her testimony with the beautiful and scriptural sentence: "I believe it because he says so." Ah! dear reader, here is the secret of victory. Believe it, not because things seem so and so, or you have or don't have certain emotional evidence, but because he said so. "The just shall live by faith"—Heb. 10:38.

> My faith looks up to Thee,
>   My faith, so small, so slow,
> It lifts its drooping eyes to see
>   And claim the blessing now.
> Thy wondrous gift it sees afar,
>   And doth not, can not fear.
>
> My faith takes hold on Thee,
>   My faith so weak, so faint,
> It lifts its trembling hands to Thee;
>   Trembling, but violent.
> The kingdom now it takes by force,
> And waits till Thou, its last resource,
>   Shall seal and sanctify.
>
> My faith holds fast on Thee,
>   My faith, still small, but sure,
> Its anchor holds alone to Thee,
>   Whose presence keeps me pure,
> By night, by day, art very near—
>   Art very near to me.

Testimony

"Ye are my witnesses, saith the Lord." "They overcame him by the blood of the Lamb, and by the word of their testimony"—Rev. 12:11.

In a meek, humble, joyful spirit, tell what the Lord has done for you. Don't shun the word "sanctification," nor any other term that the Spirit uses in designating this great work. It is God's term, and can not be improved by us. At the same time don't be in bondage to any particular one of the many phrases which abound in the Word. "Perfect love," a "pure heart," "holiness," the "single eye," "life more abundant," the "gift of the Holy Ghost," and "sanctification," are a few of the many Bible terms which may be used in testifying to the "second work of grace." It is better, however, for the benefit of those to whom you speak, to use the word "sanctification" than these others, because it is generally understood to embrace the system of truth emphasized by the holiness movement.

The devil seems to hate it more than all the rest, and as the "offense of the cross" has shifted to this despised doctrine, there is a peculiar blessing attending the clear, definite testimony to sanctification. The writer has observed that in meetings held for the promotion of holiness, where this word was studiously avoided, there was a lack of the deep, probing, heart-searching power which is so plainly manifest when the truth is preached boldly and definitely.

Hence watch, for an insidious fear of criticism may lead you to avoid this important word even before you are aware of it. Frances Willard received the blessing in Evanston, and soon after went to Lima, N.Y., to become preceptress of Genesee Wesleyan Seminary. She was advised to keep still about sanctification because of the Free Methodists in those parts. It was cruel advice. She writes: "I kept still until I soon found that I had nothing to keep still about. The experience left me…. that sweet pervasiveness, that heaven in the soul, of which I came to know in Mrs. Palmer's meetings, I do not feel" (*Holiness and Power*, 350).

Doubtless much of the effect of this sanctifying work lingered with this "uncrowned queen of America," and contributed to the phenomenal success of her life-work. However, the *fullness* of joy departed when she ceased to testify to it. Some years later she attended A. B. Simpson's meeting at Old Orchard, Me., where she received another great spiritual uplift, possibly entered again into the fullness of the sanctified life.

The sainted Fletcher lost this blessing four or five times by not testifying to it. Dr. Sheridan Baker says, "Clear testimony to full salvation is so opposed by Satan, is so distasteful to a Church, and is so much discouraged by many who are reputed wise and good, that more lose the blessing of entire sanctification by ambiguity and indefiniteness in testimony than by any other and perhaps by all other causes put together" ("Hidden Manna").

Dr. Carradine says: "Very long and sorrowful indeed is the list of preachers and laymen, men and women, who possessed the blessing of sanctification, hid the talent in a napkin, tried to live the experience, toned it down in various ways to suit family, friends, and Church, until at last they awoke to see that the star had disappeared, the angels had vanished into the skies, and the glory had departed. If we follow faithfully the divine plan of witnessing, not only with the life but the lips, certain gracious and blessed results will be felt at once to arise and increase as the days go by. One will be a sense of increased sight and gladness with every occasion of witnessing. Each time the duty is performed the Spirit will smile upon the soul well pleased. Another result will be a growing freedom, or sense of religious liberty. A third effort will be a consciously increasing strength. A fourth will be the arousing of conviction on the subject all about you. The testimony may be modestly and simply given; but if uttered clearly and unctuously, it will never fail, but hearts will be stirred and souls set to panting after this great grace of God. The song will reach the heart, the arrow will strike the mark; the testimony, in a word, will never fall to the ground. God will take care of it" ("Sanctified Life").

When family, pastor, and Church are grieved at a definite testimony, it is so natural to evade a little until the heart grows cold and the lips silent.

When the high priest entered the holy of holies he wore a garment on the borders of which hung pomegranates and bells, twelve of each alternating, the former typifying the fruitful life, the latter the testimony. First, the pomegranate of holy living, then the clear ring of the bell in witnessing. The two go hand in hand. When the bells ceased to ring the people knew that the high priest was dead. Keep the bells ringing.

Now just a word as to the manner of your testimony. The effect of a truth upon others depends largely upon whether it is wisely or unwisely stated. Therefore, instead of saying, "I am holy," say, "God has in great mercy given me a holy heart." It is preferable to say, "The very God of peace has sanctified me wholly," rather than to say, "I am sanctified." A testimony like the following will always grate on the ears and hearts of the best people: "I have not sinned in five years." How much better it would be to say: "Through the abundant grace of our Lord Jesus Christ, I have been enabled to walk before the Lord five years without condemnation!" Instead of saying, "I am perfect," say, "Be it said to the glory of God that he has perfected me in love." Direct the attention always to Jesus.

Prayer

Observe regular seasons for Bible study and secret prayer. Notwithstanding the busy toils and cares of the day, keep in close touch with God through these stated interviews, and by living constantly in the spirit of prayer. Some people rush to their knees without taking time to read the Bible, thereby losing the most effective preparation for prevailing prayer. A reverent study of the Word opens the way for the mightiest prayer. God speaks to you through the Scriptures. You speak to Him through prayer, then the blessed Holy Spirit witnesses to the word in the palace of the soul.

Take time to be alone. Make much of the still hour. Get right quiet before God. Bid all other voices be silent that he may speak to you. Sometimes we talk so hurriedly to him that he has but little chance to speak to us. Elijah did not hear the "still small voice" (or voice of gentle stillness, as it is sometimes translated) until the fire, storm, and earthquake had passed away.

"Prayer requires retirement at least of heart. Have a private place if possible, but at any event retire to the private chamber of the heart. Our closet must be in us, as well as we in our closet." Jeremy Taylor said: "A good man could build a chapel in his heart."

Abraham was closeted with God under the oak at Mamre, Jacob by the brookside, David in his bedchamber, Daniel with his window open toward Jerusalem, Peter on the housetop, and the Lord on the mountain. "Only when the heart is shut toward the world can it be open toward heaven."

Many live in such a rush that they miss that delicate finish of character, that far-reaching view of God, the massive strength, the fervid piety, the unutterable depth of love and tenderness of spirit, the triumphant faith and profound repose which are the result of frequent interviews and long communings with God. Men like Knox,

Luther, Wesley, Elijah, and John the Baptist, owed much of the heroic grandeur of their ministry to the long seasons spent in retirement with God.

Mr. Moody says that the Bible read without much prayer makes an intellectual Christian, while a great deal of prayer with but little study of the Scriptures will produce fanatical Christians. This is true. Have your own Bible, study it consecutively—that is, read it through over and over again—alternating with the study of special themes as love, faith, joy, etc. Keep yourselves prayed full. There is the gift of the Holy Spirit which you received in your sanctification, then there are many *fillings* of the Spirit which are to be sought in earnest prayer from time to time and received by simple faith. These effusions are not to be confounded with the baptism of the Holy Ghost, but are among the graces of the Spirit which are to be sought as the Lord reveals our need of them. Hence stay on your knees until you have victory. Go on to know the fullness of God. The Lord will lead you into periods of protracted, agonizing, importunate prayer. This is what the apostle calls praying in the Holy Ghost. The Spirit wrenches your soul until the cry goes up from the very marrow of your being, like a woman in travail. These are priceless occasions for then God is breathing his mighty cry through yours, and great things will follow. Study *kneeology,* for the fervent, effectual prayer of a righteous man availeth much—Jas.5:16.

Talk

"Let the words of my mouth and the meditation of my heart be acceptable in thy sight, O Lord, my strength and my redeemer"—Ps. 19:14.

Beware of a gossipy, chaffy, trashy talk. A careless, slipshod, worldly conversation will sap any one's piety. If the utterances of a single day were all written and read once in a while in connection with the evening devotions, they would furnish food for sober reflection, repentance, and prayer. Suppose that all the words you ever uttered were published in one large book. How would it read?

Society abounds in coarse, foolish, shallow, wicked conversation, which you can not indulge in without a blight on your own spirit. Then how idle and empty some people's words are! They talk, talk, talk without saying anything. All the real good in some such conversation could be entombed on the point of a cambric needle.

Let your words be seasoned with salt. Determine that through an indwelling Christ your language shall be chaste, discreet, tender, and helpful. What marvelous good can flow from a single tongue! Let your words, like the gulf stream, flow through the ocean of a wicked world only to cheer, comfort, strengthen, and bless; then the Lord will make your speech like "apples of gold in pictures of silver."

The following selection contains the gist of all that need to be said on this subject:

The Art of Governing the Tongue

"In the multitude of words there wanteth not sin"—Prov. 10:19.

"The heart of fools is in their mouth; but the mouth of the wise is in their heart"—Apocrypha.

"By thy words shalt thou be justified, and by thy words thou shalt be condemned"—Matt. 12:37.

> Choose to listen rather than to talk;
> For silence is preferable to speech.
> It is wiser to talk too little than too much:
> And to speak well than to say many things.
> Aim at speaking rather to the purpose than often.
> Reflect before speaking.
> Know how to speak by silence.
> Restrain the tongue when the heart is agitated.
> Be silent when you feel too great a desire to talk.
> Speak after others:
> Never against others;
> Always well of others; …
> Always with modesty;
> Never against the truth;
> Always with discretion: …
> When vanity has found entrance, purify the intention.
> Let your tone of voice be neither too loud nor too low….
> Never seek information through curiosity.
> Leave it to the world to talk of the world.
> Complain of nothing, neither of persons nor of things.
> Do not speak much of yourself nor of your affairs.

> Say little of your works, less of your troubles;
> Confide these to very few persons.
> Utter no useless words;
> But harmless trifles may serve you as recreation if spoken in
> God's presence and for him....

Live a Moment at a Time

Sydney Smith said: "If you would be happy, take short views of life." A greater than he said: "Be careful for nothing; but in everything by prayer and supplication with thanksgiving let your requests be made known unto God. And the peace of God, which passeth all understanding, shall keep your hearts and minds through Christ Jesus" —Phil. 4:6,7.

We borrow most of our trouble. A quaint old writer has said that God would not give grace for borrowed trouble. We are constantly climbing mountains that we never reach, crossing swollen streams which we will never see, and fearing things that will never happen. Bishop Foster says: "Acquire the habit of living by the minute. Let it not be supposed that you are not to act for the future, but act by the minute. Take care of this moment now, while you have it, and the next when it comes; you will not then neglect any. You can live this minute without sin. Is it not so? [By the help of God] do it, then. Never mind what is before you. [With the help of Jesus] do not sin now. When each successive minute comes do likewise. If you will do this, you will not sin at all. Days are made up of minutes; if each one is sinless, the day will be so. Now try this; nothing is easier, nothing is more wise. Live by the minute. Carry on your business, trade, labor, study and plan for the future by the minute. Trust in God now; do God's will now; do not offend God now. If you will observe this simple rule, you will not fail" ("Christian Purity," 262).

A. B. Earle tells us of a great merchant in new York City, with several thousand clerks, and doing an immense amount of business, who was exceedingly happy in Jesus. He was a Methodist, and had received the sanctifying Holy Ghost. Some thought he was a hypocrite on the ground that no one could do so much business and yet live so near Jesus as he appeared to do. A number formed themselves into a committee to go to his business house and watch him, that they might find some fault with his Christian life. When the clock struck he said to all who were with him, "Excuse me a minute;" and he would go into a private office, and then come back and go on with his business. The clock struck again and the act was repeated. They finally asked him what it meant. He told them that he went into that room for a word of prayer each hour. He prayed: "I thank thee, O God, that thou has kept me another hour without sin; now give me grace for the next hour." "Brethren, I serve God by the hour."

Read Holiness Literature

Keep supplied with a variety of the many excellent papers and books devoted to holiness. Merely skipping over them will not yield much profit, but thoughtful, prayerful study will find something new, stimulative, and helpful in each. If you can purchase but one book, let that be *The Christian's Secret of a Happy Life*. Next to the Bible, it is the best book that I can recommend. The gifted authoress is not so clear and radical in her doctrinal statements as some, yet it is the best book that I know of, except the Bible, to strengthen, settle, and establish you *after* you are sanctified. It is not the best book to lead you into the experience, but it will throw a flood of light on how to keep it.

Neal Dow said that Maine was carried for prohibition by sowing it down knee-deep with prohibition literature. By careful reading and wise distribution of the best holiness books and papers you can remove much of the woeful ignorance now afflicting the people on this subject.

Mind the Checks

Walk in the Spirit. When you start in the wrong direction He will gently pull the bit. You are indulging in certain conversation; suddenly there is a gentle pressure on your spirit to refrain. Mind the checks. You are pursuing certain lines of thought; there comes a mild pressure on the heart to desist. Mind the checks. You are engaged in certain transactions, when lo! "the still small voice" whispers, "Stop! *Mind the checks.*" By this means God will keep you from sin. Know his voice and instantly obey. Here is the entering wedge for so many failures. When these tender admonitions are given by the Spirit you disregard them, and backsliding begins. God grant that you may follow on to know all his fullness!

Walk in the Light

Things will be constantly coming up that you must lay aside. Possibly you did things yesterday that you can't do to-day without condemnation. Keep under the search-light of the Holy Ghost. Seek to see yourself more and more as God sees you.

Go On

You will only keep the grace you now have by going on and seeking more. There are heights, depths, and breadths in the great Father's heart that you know but little about. Press on to be filled with all his fullness—Eph. 3:19. If I had but one message to holiness people it would be, Go deeper—press on to know him in all his preciousness. Exalt him more and more until your heart is a sea of glory—a garden where all the rich graces of the Spirit bloom, a temple filled with his beauty—yea, the palace from which the royal wealth of heaven's King shall go forth to bless this old world in a thousand ways.

The Time Is Short

Do what you do quickly. Soon you will stand before the Lord. "Shall the record be found wanting?" O beloved, let your life tell mightily for God. Do your best through his strength for this poor, blind, wretched, sinful world. God grant that it may be so. Amen.

I knew that God in his Word had spoken
That the power of sin could all be broken,
The soul held captive, yet be free:
Lord, is this blessing not for me?

Must I go on in sin and sorrow,
Clouds to-day, sunshine to-morrow?
First I'm sinning, then repenting;
Now I'm stubborn, then relenting.

With anguish wrung I cried, "My God!
Is there not power in Jesus' blood
To work in me a perfect cure,
To cleanse my heart and keep it pure?"

"O yes, my love will take you in;
The blood will keep you pure within;
Will wash away your guilty stains.
And cleanse till not one spot remains."

And there I stand this very hour
Kept by almighty keeping power;
Temptations come, the blood's my plea,
The precious blood now cleanseth me.

3. A Deeper Death to Self

If McClurkan was at one with the holiness movement in areas explored in the previous selections, his emphasis on "a deeper death to self" placed him in some tension with it but kept him in touch with real life. From experience he recognized that all of life cannot be compressed into one moment of experience and offered some advice that has contemporary relevance. While one may debate the particular imagery used to describe the Christian pilgrimage, one can scarcely question his insights about this journey.

From *Wholly Sanctified*, Appendix to a later edition

For a number of years we have been associated with the holiness movement and have had the opportunity of studying it in the light of wide observation and mature thought. With the light of years have come a broadening and deepening of our grasp of this great doctrine of sanctification. We see some things more clearly than we did before, and these years of careful and prayerful study have brought additional light, some of which is set forth in the following suggestions:

1. Sanctification as set forth in this book is of a very thorough and radical type. The eradication or elimination of all sin is forcibly stressed, and thereby many have been led to clearly see that the cleansing of the heart from all sin is the very bed rock of the work wrought in sanctification, and therefore of the most vital importance. Yet we are liable, in stressing this phase of the subject, to fix the eye upon the work rather than upon the worker. This is the cause of much of the dryness which we find prevailing among holiness people. We often

say, "Do not seek an *it* or a *blessing*, but rather the *Blesser*." But even this injunction, so valuable and important, may be misleading. The *it* or cleansing should be earnestly sought, but not apart from *Him*. While the soul cries out for the blessing, take the Blesser, and lo! you have both blessing and Blesser. God is greater than any of his gifts, save the gift of himself. Stress, emphasize, fix the eye on the Giver rather than on his gifts. Lay all on the altar, throw the door of the heart wide open and receive the Sanctifier, and the sanctification will follow. Even our sanctification may be lost by continually looking at it instead of at Jesus. Get on the divine side of your consecration. Are you wholly the Lord's? Then hands off; quit meddling with God's property. So many bring their gifts to the altar, and then try to manage them. The Lord will cleanse, repair, and keep his property. Do not handle the gift after *it* has been laid on the altar. It is in the Lord's hands, and He will work in you both to will and to do of his own good pleasure. Just let him work in you all love, joy, peace, long-suffering, gentleness, goodness, faith, meekness, and temperance. Having put the old life, the good self as well as the bad, on the cross, reckon it dead according to Romans 4:11, and receive Jesus to be your wisdom, righteousness, sanctification, and redemption. *Rest* in him; the cleansing will be so precious; but most of all will be the gift of *himself* to you. Hallelujah! Here abide, and your life will be fresh, sweet, and strong for God. You can look at a blessing until a deadness and heaviness comes into the heart. You feel the lack of joy, it may be, because you are looking at an experience rather than the Lord. He is your joy. Accept him—not a *feeling*, but *Him*. He abides, hence you can "rejoice in the Lord always." May the Lord teach us more of this great truth! Thousands are pining today over an unsatisfactory experience because they are endeavoring to get it *apart* from Christ. O, receive him to be all and in all!

The sanctified life is described in its fullness in this volume. That many professors of holiness do not fully reach this high standard, we freely admit. What shall be done about it? Lower the standard? No; but strive to bring the people up to it. There are several reasons why so many fail to live the life in its fullness. Some are only regenerated or reclaimed, and as a matter of course they do not live a sanctified life on the experience of conversion only. Others went far enough to receive a great spiritual uplift, but did not fully enter the Canaan life. Then others, though sanctified, allowed the unfriendly criticism of the church, the world, the flesh, and the devil to so impede their progress that they either lost their sanctification or were shorn of its power. As in the regenerated life there are different degrees, so in this. Some merely cross the Jordan; others go to Jericho; while still others, in their zeal to possess all the land, go far up into the mountains of the Canaan life. Entering the sanctified life is but the beginning of the full-orbed normal Christian career. There are many of God's dear children, among the number some beautiful characters, who never grasp the life of godliness in its deeper and higher phases.

Again, some of the portraits which we have sketched of the sanctified life belong to its maturer stages. At this point the wisest discrimination is needed to avoid confounding purity with maturity. A baby is as perfect a human being as a man, but it is not as mature. So in the life of holiness this same distinction must be observed if we would avoid erroneous conclusions. Through consecration and faith a pure heart is obtained and the sanctified life begins. Then there are infinite depths and heights lying beyond, into which we must press if we retain the fire and live the life in its fullness. So many fail to press eagerly on into these deeper things, and thereby lose at least the fullness and completeness of a holy life.

2. Thousands have been hindered for want of a clear statement of the real work wrought in sanctification. Sufficient emphasis has not been laid upon

A Deeper Death to Self

In sanctification we die to sin; in this deeper death we die to self. "The very largest degrees of self-renovation, crucifixion, and abandonment to God take place after the work of heart purity." *Higher* and *deeper* should be our motto. A higher appreciation and grasp on divine things, with a deeper death to self, is the present need of the holiness movement—higher in the sense of having tons more of love, joy, peace, long-suffering, gentleness, goodness, faith, meekness, and temperance; deeper in that we die more thoroughly to our own ways, plans, ideas, preferences, likes, and dislikes. We might say that there is a *sinful* self and a *natural* self. Sanctification delivers from the former, while the latter "dies daily." For instance, Peter was a sanctified man when that sheet was let down before him, but he was not free from traditional theology nor race prejudice. The sanctified man is saved from everything that he *sees* to be wrong, but the "ego" or creature life still exists, and displacement of the natural self by the incoming of the Christ life is the work accomplished in these deeper crucifixions. We must die to many things not in themselves sinful, but they are weights and hindrances in the soul's flight toward God, and should be laid aside.

The following quotations from that excellent book *"Soul Food"* will be found very helpful:

"In contradistinction from heart cleansing, this finer crucifixion of self is gradual; it extends through months or years. The interior spirit is mortified over and over on the same point till it reaches a state of divine indifference to it."

"A great host of believers have obtained heart purity, and yet for a long time have gone through all sorts of 'dying daily' to self before they found that calm, fixed union with the Holy Ghost which is the deep longing of the child of God."

Job was a perfect man, and yet he had to die to his religious self— the good Job—and he died very hard. This death to our *good selves* seems to us to be the crowning lesson in the book of Job.

"Again, in contradistinction from heart cleansing, which is by faith, this deeper death to self is by suffering…. There are literally scores of Scripture passages like Psalm 71:19-21, teaching that the upper ranges in the sanctified state are wrought out through suffering. Perhaps the most remarkable passage of the Word on this subject is in the fifth chapter of Romans. The first verse teaches justification by faith, the second verse teaches full salvation by faith, and verses three, four and five teach a deeper death and fuller Holy Ghost life by tribulation."

"When the soul undergoes this deeper death to self it enters into a great wideness of spiritual comprehension and love, a state of almost uninterrupted prayer; of boundless charity for all people; of unutterable tenderness and broadness of sympathy; of deep, quiet thoughtfulness; of extreme simplicity of life and manners, and of deep vision of God and the coming ages."

Sanctified suffering crucifies self and gives a more delicate touch and finer shades of character to the spirit. It "*gives a great wideness to the heart* and a universality of love." "It destroys that littleness and narrowness of mind" so manifest in many good people. It equips the soul "with an inexpressible *tenderness.*" It is the very tenderness of Jesus filling the thoughts, the feelings, the manners, the words, the tones of the voice; the whole being is soaked in a sea of gentleness. Everything hard, bitter, severe, critical, flinty, has been crushed into powder. Great sufferers have been noted for their quiet gentleness. As we approach them it is like going to a tropical climate in mid-winter. The very air around them seems mellow; their slow, quiet words are like the gentle ripple of summer seas on the sand; their soft, pathetic eyes put a hush upon our rudeness or loudness of voice. There are many souls who are earnest Christians—nay, many who are sanctified—who have an indescribable something in them which needs the crushing and melting of some great crucifixion. Their tongues rattle so much, their spirit is dictatorial or harsh, they measure other people by themselves, there is something in their constitution which seems to need the grinding into finer flour, and that something, I might add, is the "ego" or natural self life. This crucifixion is the work-ing out in every detail and minutia of life all the principles of self-renunciation involved in the consecration. "Our lofty reason, our brightest hopes, our cherished affections, our religious views, our dear-est friendship, our pious zeal, our spiritual impetuosity, our success, our religions, our spiritual comforts," need to pass through this finer crucifixion until we are dead to all but God.

Sanctified people, you cannot live a holy life on the plane of last year's experience! You will only keep what you have by pressing on to know Him better. Let there be no loitering by the way. Child of heaven, run like a swift courier toward the skies! We must press forward into these deeper experiences, or many will become narrow, harsh, and intolerant, which is simply "sour holiness." The conviction has been growing on us for years that the only way by which we can hold what we have already obtained is by going on into these deeper crucifixions and knowing more of "the fellowship of his sufferings," if by any means we might be "made conformable unto his death." Let the watchword of each be, *forward, higher, deeper!* Let us rise on the "stepping stones of our dead selves" into the bosom of God. Amen.

Second Coming Of Christ

J. O. McClurkan's book on the Second Coming of Christ was entitled *Behold He Cometh: A Series of Brief Lessons on the Second Coming of Christ.* In the introduction he describes the book as "a brief, clear, and comprehensive statement of the generally accepted teaching of those who believe that the coming of the Lord draweth nigh. There is not a great deal of originality in the book. It is chiefly a compilation of premillennial teaching…. The author's purpose is to… state, in a condensed way, some of the best thoughts of those who are more competent to speak on this subject." Therefore, the book represents the teaching of premillennial dispensationalism which was in its heyday at the time, but which has subsequently undergone significant modifications by those who subscribe to this teaching. The following selection includes selected passages from chapter 12, "The Practical Effect of This Doctrine."

From *Behold He Cometh*, Chapter 12, selected passages

"Every man that hath this hope in him, purifieth himself even as he is pure"

—*1 John 3:3.*

One of the ablest and most godly of America's great preachers said some time ago, that there had been three great epochs in his life. First when he was regenerated; second, when he received the gift of the Holy Ghost; third, when he saw the blessed truth of the Lord's coming. God is an economist. He reveals just what we need, nothing more, nor nothing less than what is necessary, for the development of the very highest type of Christian character. The marked prominence given to this important theme throughout the Word of God indicates that it is of first importance. It is the keystone in the arch of scriptural truth; the individual Christian or church that neglects to stress this doctrine will lose much….

The failure to stress the second coming of Christ has always ended in apostasy. Take our modern Protestantism, rich, worldly, and proud of which the saintly and venerable Bishop Foster says, "Just now four out of five of our church rolls are doing nothing, almost absolutely nothing; and God's blessed cause is not made one whit stronger in numbers or influence by their living. The Church of God is to-day courting the world. Its members are bringing it down to the level of the ungodly...."

[Belief in the imminent return of Christ] stimulates every phase of Christian life.

1. There is no other truth which will bring more conviction to the unsaved. The thought that Jesus is coming soon, and that he may appear at any moment, produces serious, anxious inquiry among the ungodly.

2. It is an incentive to holiness. Every man that hath this hope in him, purifieth himself even as he is pure—1 John 3:3. The very God of peace sanctify you wholly; and I pray God your whole spirit and soul and body be preserved blameless unto the coming of our Lord Jesus Christ—1 Thess. 5:23.

"Seeing then that all these things shall be dissolved, what manner of persons ought we to be in all holy conversation and godliness, looking for and hasting unto the coming (or hastening the coming) of the day of God, wherein the heavens being on fire shall be dissolved, and the elements shall melt with fervent heat? Nevertheless, we, according to his promise, look for new heavens and a new earth wherein dwelleth righteousness. Wherefore, beloved, seeing that ye look for such things, be diligent, that ye may be found of him in peace, without spot and blameless." Also Titus 2:12-14.

A church looking for Jesus to return will not be mixed up in any kind of worldliness. Wherever this doctrine is received and properly recognized, the line between the Church and the world is clearly drawn. The movement for the "deepening" of the Christian life, now extending throughout all Christendom, is the preparation of the Bride, for holiness will be her trousseau. When she has been made ready then Christ will return, catch her away in the clouds, and the following announcement will be proclaimed: "The marriage of the Lamb has come, and his wife hath made herself ready. And to her was granted that she should be arrayed in fine linen, clean and white, for the fine linen is the righteousness of saints."

3. It provokes to zeal. "The night is far spent, the day is at hand."

"Behold, I come quickly, and my reward is with me, even to give to every man according as his work shall be."

"Hold fast that that thou hast, that no man take thy crown." The most indefatigable workers are those who have fallen into harmony with God's plan, and are pressing forward animated by the blessed hope that "the coming of the Lord draweth nigh." They are no more sluggards in the vineyard, for the Master may appear at any moment....

4. It leads to a real yearning for the Lord to return. "Even so, Lord Jesus, come quickly." We have read somewhere the story of a maiden whose lover was lost at sea. Night after night, for day after day, for year after year, she sat with a light in her little cottage window by the seaside peering out over the dark, restless waves, with a hope that maybe he would return. So the Christian looks out over the endless waste of iniquity about him, up to the skies above, from whence he knows the Lord will appear. The bridegroom does not come until the bride is attired for the wedding. When the Church gets robed and ready, the cry will sound forth, "Behold the Bridegroom cometh, go ye out to meet him." Reader, did it ever occur to you that it was possible to hasten his coming? One reason for the long delay is that his people have not longed for him. If there is anything else that we prefer to his advent, we are not fully prepared to greet him with the whole hearted welcome which he should have....

5. It keeps us close to him. "And now, little children, abide in him, that when he shall appear we may have confidence, and not be ashamed at his coming." As A. B. Simpson says: "When Elisha knew that Elijah's translation was near, he kept very close to his side. To every suggestion that he should leave his side he answered, 'As the Lord thy God liveth, and as thy soul liveth, I will not leave thee.' So, if we are waiting and watching for his coming, we will not let a moment separate us from him. It was but one evening that Thomas was absent, but that very evening Jesus came. So let us cling to his side that his coming shall be no surprise, for the master himself is already within our happy heart, 'the hope of glory.'"

6. It is an incentive to patience. "Therefore judge nothing before the time, until the Lord come, who will both bring to light the hidden things of darkness, and will make manifest the counsels of the hearts; and then shall every man have praise of God." "Be patient, therefore,

brethren, unto the coming of the Lord. Behold, the husbandman waiteth for the precious fruit of the earth, and hath long patience for it, until he receive the early and the latter rain. Be ye also patient; stablish your hearts; for the coming of the Lord draweth nigh."

"Let your moderation be known to all men. Be careful (anxious) for nothing." The wicked will soon cease from troubling. All these hardships, toils, and battles are but for a moment. They can only last till Jesus comes, and that may occur to-day.

> A few more struggles here,
> A few more partings o'er,
> A few more toils, a few more tears,
> And we shall weep no more.

7. It promotes heavenly mindedness. "It is like Dr. Chalmers' famous picture of the inhabitants of a pestilential marsh, who had again and again been urged to emigrate, but they could not be induced to leave a certain for an uncertain good. At last one day they saw approaching and slowly passing by a beauteous isle, clothed with a verdure and loveliness they had never seen before, and breathing the balmy air of its glad and eternal spring over all their unhealthy plains. Then they began to eagerly inquire if they might enter its blessed harbor. They sent out their boats across the sea, they entreated permission to land upon the shores, and they gladly let go their old cabins and treasures, and hastened to the happy shores of this bright and holy Paradise."

The man who lives in daily anticipation of these eternal joys will hold this world with a light grasp. Now he is a stranger and a pilgrim, but when Jesus comes he will enter in his glory.

8. It gives hope to the bereaved. "But I would not have you to be ignorant, brethren, concerning them which are asleep, that ye sorrow not, even as others which have no hope. For the Lord himself shall descend from heaven with a shout, with the voice of the archangel and with the trump of God, and the dead in Christ shall rise first. Then we which are alive and remain, shall be caught up to meet the Lord in the air; and so shall we ever be with the Lord." Wherefore comfort one another with these words. No doubt when Jesus comes, some of his people will be dying, but death will flee away; others will

be on the road to the cemetery, when the trump of God sounds, the funeral will be suddenly broken up, for they will spring out of their caskets, as he did out of Joseph's tomb that Sabbath morning. Others, while the graves are being filled will come forth with a shout of victory. Your loved ones may rise even before you leave the grave. One thing is sure, they will come forth clad, not in the habilaments of death (the grave clothes will all be left behind), but in robes of light and victory, they will go forth to greet their Lord. There is no record of Christ meeting a funeral while here on earth that he did not break it up. Death could not stand in his presence. Jesus conquered him long ago. After awhile we can stand at the mouth of every vacant tomb and shout, "There shall be no more death." Hallelujah.

> The dead in Christ shall first arise,
>   At the last trumpet's sounding—
> Caught up to meet him in the skies,
>   With joy their Lord surrounding.

9. It is a powerful factor in promoting missionary zeal. They, who are looking for him to appear, erelong, in the clouds of heaven, are hastening to send the gospel to the pagan world. Ah! How we have played at missions! What awful indifference. What if a population twice that of Boston die every week without having heard of Christ, or that annually the number equals that of the British Isles? What matters the twenty-five millions of child widows in India, the horrible atrocities of the African slave trade, the girl babies left on the streets to die in China, the tens of thousands of innocent girls dedicated in the name of religion to a life of shame; the brutal treatment of prisoners, most of them probably innocent; the wholesale degradation of women; the countless millions of lost souls! A drowsy, sluggish church pays little heed to these things. They are living in reckless disregard of their obligations to the heathen. One hundred thousand who never heard of Christ die every day, while the women of America pay far more for artificial flowers for their hats and bonnets, than the entire Church of God gives to missions. The tobacco bill of America for one year, is larger than the entire contribution for the spread of the gospel during the past eighteen centuries. There is spent for whisky in two days as much as the church pays for missions in twelve months.

It is estimated that there is ten times as much spent for rings, and eighteen times as much for jewelry, as flows into all the missionary treasuries of the world. The extra buttons which the American women put on their kid gloves is double the offering of the world for missions. The wealth of the church members in this country runs way up into the millions, their annual savings being estimated as high as five hundred millions of dollars, with a missionary contribution of fifty cents per capita. It is indeed a shameful and humiliating state of affairs.

But a sanctified, spirit-filled church is essentially a flame of missionary zeal....

10. It is a trumpet call to watchfulness; "Watch ye, therefore, for ye know neither the day nor the hour when the Son of Man cometh." "Let your loins be girded about, and your lights burning, and ye [yourselves] like unto men who watch for the Lord when he will return from the wedding, that when he cometh and knocketh, they may open to him immediately. Blessed are those servants whom the Lord when he cometh shall find watching. Of a truth I say unto you that he shall gird himself, and make them sit down to meat, and will come forth and serve them. And if he shall come in the second watch or come in the third watch, and find them so, blessed are those servants. And this know, that if the good man of the house had known what hour the thief would come he would have watched, and would not have suffered his house to be broken through. Be ye also ready, therefore, for the Son of Man cometh at an hour when ye think not."

The only sure way to be ready is to be in the line of obedience, and watching continually lest he come upon you unawares. "For, unto them that look for him, will he appear the second time, without sin unto salvation."

McCheyne, the Scotch preacher, once said to some friends, "Do you think Christ will come tonight?" One after another they said, "I think not." When all had given this answer, he solemnly repeated this text: "The Son of Man cometh at an hour *when ye think not.*"

The Lord help us, to so live, that we will not be surprised when he appears.

Urgency Of Mission

The "Eleventh Hour Concept" was a significant influence in McClurkan's theology. With its belief in the imminent return of Christ, this concept contributed an urgency to the mission to be carried out by evangelism, foreign missions, and education. The following selection is taken from chapter 21, "The Eleventh Hour Laborers," of McClurkan's book *Chosen Vessels,* and reflects his commitment to the "Eleventh Hour Concept." This chapter was also published in *Zion's Outlook* (March 7, 1901).

From *Chosen Vessels*, Chapter 21

Rev. F. L. Chappell, who recently fell asleep in Jesus, has written a little book under the... caption [*The Eleventh Hour Laborers*], which is unique and strikingly suggestive, and we are inclined to believe that the explanation of the origin and purpose of the various Pentecostal movements of the day are clearly stated in this book. He says:

"If our Lord's parables cover the whole dispensation, as some excellent interpreters suppose; and if we are nearing the end of the dispensation, the eleventh hour laborers, mentioned in Matt. 20:5,6, may represent a class hitherto unemployed, but now called into service because of the urgency of the work during the closing days."

The call at the third, sixth and ninth hours is more ordinary and normal, since these are the common greater divisions of the day which laborers are wont to observe. But rarely do we ever hear of workmen being engaged for only the last hour of the day. The action of the householder is unusual and may represent the urgent need of hitherto unemployed laborers as the dispensation is closing.

And is this not the meaning of much that we are now beholding? Certainly a class of Christian laborers hitherto unemployed are by some power being urged into the work. And can we deny that they come at the call of the Master? Do they not work with a zeal corresponding to the urgency of the time? Faith missions, special missions, personal missions, independent missions, undenominational missions, etc., are now added to the old-time and long-time methods of evangelization. They do not supersede those in the field before them any more than the bicycle supersedes the use of horses and carriages; but simply meet the more urgent demand of the swift going times.

But if the Lord of the vineyard pays these last first; and gives them equal reward with those in the field before them, are they not precious in his estimation? And are not their labors worthy of special attention?

Some Principal Groups

The China Inland Mission, organized thirty years ago by J. Hudson Taylor, has six or eight hundred missionaries, who are laboring heroically for the evangelization of that great empire. The Salvation Army, under the direction of General Booth, is reaching out in every direction after the fallen. The Christian and Missionary Alliance, led by A. B. Simpson, is belting the globe with mission stations. The East London Institute Mission, managed by H. Grattan Guinness, has now more than six hundred missionaries in the field, and are sending out others at the rate of one per week. The work in South Africa, under the leadership of Andrew Murray, Peniel Mission, led by Mrs. Manie Fergurson, with scores of similar enterprises, too numerous to mention, all belong to the eleventh hour movement.

Their Equipment

The eleventh hour laborer is called at the *last* hour; hence his equipment for the work is peculiar. The urgency of the case demands "shortcut" methods in preparing for the work. Training schools, Bible institutes, etc., are springing up all over the country.

Notwithstanding the criticisms hurled at these schools, they have come to stay. They are an essential part of the eleventh hour work. They stress three points: 1. God reigning in you—the Baptism of the Holy Spirit. 2. The Bible in the heart for the sword in the hand. 3. Practical work, by laboring in missions, street meetings, evangelistic tours, etc. They go, Bible in hand, anointed with the Spirit.

Their Message

"Repent, for the kingdom of heaven is at hand." Men are bidden to prepare for the coming of Jesus. Repentance and conversion for the sinner, and sanctification with the fullness of the Spirit for the believer —these two themes constitute the burden of their ministry. It does not require so much preparation to effectively declare these great truths, provided the cloven tongue has been given. In fact, these truths are uttered by the eleventh hour laborers with more telling effect than by any other class of workers. We have seen uneducated, frail women, filled with the Spirit, more powerful in winning souls than half a dozen cultured doctors of divinity.

Their Literature

There is an expectant, aggressive, exultant note in their literature indicating the stirring character of their work. Notice some of the names of their papers, such as, "Age to Come Herald," "Coming Age," "Herald of Life," "Herald of Salvation," "Herald of Holiness," "Messiah's Herald," "Faithful Witness," "Holiness Evangelist," "Times of Refreshing," "Regions Beyond," "Warning Cry," etc. The rapid increase of this type of literature within the past few years is profoundly suggestive. Some of it is distributed gratuitously, and almost all of it is the heart cry of little companies of devout, choice, fragrant spirits, here and there. This kind of spiritual food has become a necessity, and is largely read by hungry souls. The holiness literature of the day reads much like the New Testament. Thank God for the rich spiritual food given us by the eleventh hour movement.

Their Songs

The character and mission of a people is clearly seen in their songs for they are but the voice of the heart. There is an absence in eleventh hour music of the heavy, sombre and sad. The eleventh hour music is as noisy as the deafening shouts that rose beneath the walls of Jericho as they marched seven times in succession around it. Please observe that much of the last day was spent in marching and shouting. Many of God's dear children believe that they discover the advancing rays of the Sun of Righteousness coming over the eastern hills, and that the Jericho of sin will soon fall before King Immanuel; hence, as Brother Chappell says, "A kind of disorderly exuberance has seized the believing ones, as in faith they fill up the part assigned to them, and shout and sing and pray in view of what their God is about to do. The time for orderly marching and solemnly waiting is nearly over, and the time of tumultuous victory is close at hand, or, to change the figure, it is no longer the sowing in tears, but the reaping in joy that is now in order. Hence, the almost hilarious songs of the reapers are following so closely upon the former sad tears of the sowers, yea more, almost mingling together. Bear with them, then, even if they seem rather incongruous. The unusual trumpetings and shoutings seemed proper enough when the walls had fallen. But the instinct of faith multiplied its expression before the fact."

Women Witnessing

One of the peculiarities of the eleventh hour movement is the emphasis it places on woman's work. "The women that publish the glad tidings are a great host." Quiet, humble girls are being called into the work, and the Spirit is resting mightily upon the "daughters" and "handmaidens," according to Joel's prophecy. Just as when an emergency arises the women are pressed into service, like housing a harvest on the farm when a storm is seen approaching, or helping to save goods from a house on fire, so their call is thought to be the result of an emergency movement, to give the world its final call.

Their Convocations

Conventions, institutes, campmeetings, etc., are a necessary part of the eleventh hour work. Meetings for the deepening of the Christian life, for learning more about "his glorious appearing," for stirring up fervent missionary interest, etc., are dotting the whole land. Step into any of them, and you will find a body of earnest, thoughtful Christians, discussing such themes as "Holiness," "The Coming of the Lord," "The Regions Beyond," and kindred subjects. The unity of the Spirit is clearly manifest in these gatherings; for denominationalism is not mentioned, though nearly every sect is represented. More important questions are engaging their attention than the issues on which most denominations differ. They are getting ready for "the gathering together unto him."

Their Tabernacles

Believing as they do that they are an "emergency force," called to give the world its final warning, preparatory to the return of the Lord, they do not attach great importance to the brick and mortar feature of the work, choosing to expend their energies in soul saving, rather than in the erection of costly church edifices. They are a people of tabernacles, tents, old warehouses, brush arbors and open-air meetings.

Missionary Zeal

They literally go everywhere, preaching the word. The gift of the Holy Spirit, according to Acts 1:8, sends them to the uttermost parts of the earth. Missions are no longer a dead letter with them, and there will be no abatement of their tireless zeal, until the last tribe and nation has heard the gospel. Not only do they give their money, but they give *themselves* to this work. They will either go in person to the heathen lands, or send someone else.

Their Faces

The celestial fires which burn in the soul are usually reflected in the face. A shrewd observer can generally distinguish the eleventh hour laborer by the expression of the countenance. There is a restful, hopeful and oftentimes joyful and unearthly glow about their faces that cannot but impress the close observer. A certain lady said to her husband, as he returned from church, "I know you are sanctified, because you look just like those holiness people." Whence cometh this far away look, this supernatural touch? Evidently it is from the Christ enthroned within.

Their Testings

They are a peculiarly tried people. The devil, the flesh, the world and many formal church members combine to crush them. Their aggressive and holy lives are a constant rebuke to the world. Satan attacks them in subtle and fierce ways, unknown to many who are not living in the "heavenlies," but in the midst of it all they are hid in the secret of His pavilion, and kept from the strife of tongues, and are coming forth out of these furnace experiences with a "deeper death to self," and a sweeter and more conscious union with Christ. The furnace takes only the dross away, and puts the heavenly "shine" on them.

Their Base of Supplies

They go to the Lord for everything. "My soul, wait thou only upon God; for my expectation is from him," expresses their attitude. Hence, [they have] various institutions supported by faith.

We might speak of the swiftness of their movements, the intensity of their efforts for souls, according to Jude 23, and various other characteristics, suggested by Brother Chappell's line of thought; but already this article has gone beyond the usual length. Suffice it to say that agencies, methods and means are being pressed into service in these closing days that could not have been so effectively used in the past, but are now among the mighty forces used in dealing the final blow against the power of darkness, and ushering in the millennial reign.

Personal Evangelism

J. O. McClurkan wrote on no subject with more passion than on the subject of personal evangelism. No doubt this emphasis results from his own love for this aspect of discipleship and his effectiveness in doing it. In the introduction to McClurkan's book *Personal Work*, President Ira Landrith of Ward-Belmont College (now Belmont University) wrote these words about McClurkan: "Like our Master, whom he unselfishly serves, he goes about doing good; and obeying the behest of that Master, he goes even out into the highways and hedges and constrains men and women to come in to the feast the Lord hath spread. He daily does personal work, not alone by inviting the ungodly to accept Christ, but by Christlike ministries of mercy and love to the bodies, minds and souls of God's poor, and therefore our poor."

From *Personal Work*, selected passages

Most people are agreed that personal work ought to be done, and in a general way will indicate that they feel they ought to be doing more than they are, but there is the lack of anything like a determined, persistent purpose to do it. The conviction is not deep enough to result in such a strong will-force as to overcome all obstacles. Much indifference is due to the fact that people have not *looked* upon the fields. They have a kind of hazy, indefinite idea of the needs of the field, but it has never gripped them…

We need what the old fathers called a "burden for souls" such as caused Whitefield to exclaim, "Give me souls or take my soul." Matthew Henry said, "I would think it a greater happiness to gain one soul for Christ than mountains of silver and gold for myself;" and Doddridge said, "I long for the conviction of souls more than for anything besides." John Welch would get out of bed on cold winter nights and throw his Scotch robe around him and pour out his soul in fervent prayer, exclaiming, "I have the souls of three thousand to answer for, while I know not how it is with them;" and the sainted Brainerd, who literally burned out with zeal, cried out, "I care not where I live nor what hardships I endure so that I may gain souls for Christ." There is an alarming absence of the *groan* in much of our modern ministry. It has been our privilege to hear a number of bright, and very interesting addresses to ministers from talented men during the past few years, and if we were to make any criticism it would be the absence of that thing that would send the preachers to their knees. There was no groan. The Calvary message must be preached in the spirit of Calvary else it becomes a mere professionalism. Judged by this rule, how much of our work is but as "sounding brass and tinkling cymbal"?

The needs are appalling. The fields are still white unto the harvest, and the laborers are few. The Lord is seeking avenues through which he can reach these neglected ones. He wants to use your eyes to see the need, your ears to hear the call, your feet to go on His errands, and your hands through which to work. He wants your heart through which to love. In other words he wants the whole man yielded to Him that the life of Christ may be lived over again in you. Yonder is a man that needs to be touched, but God wants you to touch him. Yonder is a man who needs to be loved, but God wants to pour His love through you. Yonder is a man who needs to be saved, but God wants to save him through you. He reaches one man through another man. That is the divine plan. Here is a great company to be reached. Who will volunteer to be a channel through whom God can pour himself into the people?

A life lived for God is the largest and richest investment possible. The glory of a life lived for others is only realized by those noble souls who give themselves unto the Lord....

The unused talent, tied up in napkins and hid away is cursing the church. People are starving in their own souls because of this self-centeredness, and the world at large is suffering great loss on account of it. There is enough latent force within the church to evangelize the world within the next ten years if it could only all be used. There are tongues silent who might speak the glories of grace beyond the utterance of any angel. There are hands idle that could, under the touch of the Spirit, bring to pass mighty things. There are eyes blinded that anointed by the salve of the skies could peer into the glories of redemption so as to enrapture others with the story. There are ears closed that touched by the divine finger could be opened to hear things that no one else has heard, but this vast unused force has clogged the stream of the activity of the church, and has so checked her progress as to largely paralyze her efficiency.

How to Begin

Follow me, and I will make you fishers of men—Matt. 4:19.

He first findeth his own brother Simon.... And he brought him to Jesus—John 1:41,42.

Andrew never parleyed about how to reach Simon, but simply went and brought him to Jesus. The best way in the world to begin is to begin. Rotherham's translation of the Master's words to the woman who anointed Him was, "What she had she used." Her gifts may not have been large or varied, but out of a heart full of the most ardent devotion she poured what she had, and it won from the heart of Jesus an encomium that will ring down through the church as long as time will last. Begin with what you have. It may be only the five loaves and two fishes, such as the lad possessed. It may seem so little for such a great multitude, but when it is all yielded to the Lord it will be wonderfully multiplied....

Don't try to be anybody else, but consecrate to God your own talent and the power will be forthcoming, for whatever He calls you to do. Some people have a strange idea of power....

Perhaps you may make mistakes, but who hasn't? The man who never makes a mistake, as a rule, is a man who has never done any-thing. Seek the Lord for guidance. He will show you your work. It will hardly be in an audible voice, nor marked out before you just like a railroad track; but there will be a drift or bias in your soul, a certain bent in your spirit that tells you that is the thing you ought to do, an inner feeling of oughtness, a gentle whisper within, saying: "This is the way, walk ye in it."

There are many kinds of personal work. There are many ways to reach men. All are not called to the same particular kind of work, nei-ther [is] all equally gifted, but there are none more insignificant, none more obscure than the lad who had that that was used to feed the hungry multitude in the olden time. Matthew Simpson, of whom there was none more eloquent in all the church, said that he had just begun to talk as a boy and he was surprised later on to hear the people call such humble effort sermons. The secret was this: he poured out what the Lord gave him in such an impassioned way that the people could not be other than deeply impressed. He began....

Begin enthusiastically. That is one of the secrets of success. It is hard to do much with a discouraged man. This is one reason why young Moody succeeded so well. He was full of a God-given enthusiasm. He could barely read as he had had only meager advantages, but he loved God and souls and while clerking in a shoe store in Chicago, he found ample time to outdo all others in personal work....

Approach people as if you expect them to be glad that you are doing so. Give them the great facts of the gospel with as much eagerness as you would hand them hidden treasure. Put your soul into it. Let your very spirit go out into your words and move them....

Be bold. Someone has said that the modern church is lacking in initiative and boldness of undertaking. This is true. Boldness is not some loud-mouthed, coarse-faced, egotistical thing, but it is a certain attitude of spirit born with an assurance that you are sent of God, and this gives a tone of authority that compels a hearing. Not assumed authority. Forced leadership repels people. Ezekiel was assured that although the people might not yield and be obedient to his message, yet they should know that a prophet had been in their midst. The church must have this tone of authority, and does it not come from contact with Him who spoke as one having authority, and not as the scribes and Pharisees? There is all the difference in the message of the Divinely credentialed man and the whimperings of an ecclesiastical time-server. The one has the lightning of the skies and the other the flickering candle of human authority. Boldness is peculiarly linked with gentleness and meekness. The most successful workers have found their strength in quietness and confidence. They are not running over the country asserting themselves, but as heaven's appointed evangelists they are pouring forth that glad song of redemption....

There is great power in testimony. All Christians are called to witness for the Lord, and commonplace as it may seem, a testimony that comes from anointed lips never loses its impressiveness. Witnessing is one department of Christian work from which none [is] debarred. The opportunities will be continually occurring and the privilege of testifying to the riches of grace is priceless. Inviting people to the services is not an unimportant thing. Many have been reached through a simple beginning like this. They must hear the gospel if it is to effect them. Begin now, the Spirit will lead. Enter the first door, and there you will find the Lord ready to bless....

Necessary Equipment

Every personal worker should have a clean life. The righteousness movement needs added emphasis. There are well-meaning people who are so lacking in ethical discernment that they cause others to stumble. The perfect life may be considered a thing impossible, but nothing less than this will meet the requirement that the world makes of a Christian. Study to know what the right is, and then through Divine grace do it. Poor living accounts for much barrenness in personal work. To reach others we must have their confidence....

People resent being approached on the subject of salvation by those in whom they have little confidence. They look upon it as a bit of hypocrisy and they harden under it. Schwartz, the apostolic missionary who toiled in India for nearly forty years, living a life of marked self-denial and poverty, but walking among the people with a pure heart and clean hands, so won their confidence that when trouble would arise between the natives and the English, these heathen people who dared not trust government officials would say, "Send for Schwartz...."

Have confidence in the vitality of the message. The personal worker is a sower going forth to sow. He is to sow beside all waters. There is always good ground. If the soul-winner has no confidence in the message himself, how can he expect others to have it. It is astonishing how the enemy has succeeded in weakening the faith of Christian people in the vitality of the word. They will use it freely and then talk as if it is uncertain about any good being accomplished. Some seem to have forgotten that He has said: "My word shall not return unto Me void, but it shall accomplish that which he pleaseth, and prosper in the thing whereunto it is sent." Every worker should have enough Scripture in hand to apply when needed. It is not necessary to delay till one is a Bible scholar. An earnest spirit, coupled with a limited knowledge of the Scriptures, may accomplish more, but each should "study to show himself approved unto God, a workman that needeth not to be ashamed, rightly dividing the word of truth," and giving to each his portion in due season. This requires constant Bible study.

There are scriptures bearing upon every need, and while beginners may not have them all in hand, they should have at their fingers' end enough to begin with, and the Word should be quoted with absolute assurance as to its power. Remember that the Spirit is present to vitalize it and to quicken the heart of the hearer. Use it confidently and believe continuously as you are doing so that the Spirit is applying the truth. Happy the worker that has discovered that as he works God works. It may be as he preaches or kneels by the bedside of the sick or speaks a passing word to someone on the highway. God is blessing him. There is a spiritual force that impresses it. It is well to think of ourselves as conductors of these heaven-given messages. Just as the wire bears the electric current around the earth, so we are channels through which the Spirit conveys blessing to others. Recognizing this fact, we can touch people with the assurance that God touches through us. This brings such a restfulness of heart and such an assurance of success that the personal worker is thrilled with the possibilities wrapped up in even one act. The Lord Jesus frequently quoted the Scriptures as His weapon of defense. He never questioned their authenticity, genuineness or power, and He always spoke as one having authority....

Prayer

J. O. McClurkan was above all a man of prayer. He prayed in the offices of the businessmen, on the street, in the homes of the people, in the hospitals with the sick and dying, and as he went about the duties of a busy day. Prayer was a vital part of his spiritual life. Most of his prayers were brief "thumbnail prayers." He called them "short, terse, heartfelt petitions that drove straight to the core of the need without allowing time for extraneous circumstances to break in upon the privacy of the moment." The following selections from McClurkan's book *The Ministry of Prayer* should inspire all of us to take seriously our prayer life and to recognize that "the school of prayer is one from which no one ever graduates." We can all pray with the apostles, "Lord, teach us to pray."

From *The Ministry of Prayer*, selected passages

The Prayer Life

Some pray hurriedly, some spasmodically, some methodically, and some not at all. He who succeeds in getting people to pray is a benefactor indeed. In the multitudinous forms of religious service prayer is often neglected. Any religious movement that fails to deepen the prayer life is deficient. Recognizing all the good in modern evangelism, we are forced to admit that it often lacks that profound grip on the inner man that crystallizes in the prayer habit. We verily believe that to pray well is better than to preach well, and certain are we that he who prays right will live right. There is no surer test of a man's spirituality than his prayer life. Public prayer, on certain occasions, affords excellent opportunities for human exploitations and gratifying the pomp and "strut of the flesh," but private prayer brings one face to face with God, and is a character test. The lip-service worshipper can address eloquent prayers to the audience, but in the secret place his mouth is shut.

The age is not favorable to the prayer life. People are borne along on the current with a rush. Times are strenuous. To take time to pray requires more courage now than it did in the more slow-going days of our fathers.

One of the best ways to learn how to pray is to pray. Each prayer life must take shape according to the individual surroundings and needs. We cannot lay down a specific rule for all. We learn more how to pray by praying than by any other way. We may err in insisting too much on detail, but there are suggestions of a general nature that are helpful.

Have a place for prayer—not such a slavish adherence to it that you cannot pray anywhere else, but simply a Bethel or Peniel—a prayer workshop. People have a place to sleep, a place to eat, and a place for everything else in the general run of affairs; why not have a place for prayer? There is something in a *place* where you may be free from interruptions and be shut in with God. The Lord Jesus sought such quietude during His arduous ministry—places like the mountaintop, where He could be alone with the Father. His was a crowded ministry, and He needed the retirement such as these scenes of solitude afforded. All our praying is not to be done at a certain place, but it is well to have a prayer chamber for regular, systematic worship.

The Psalmist said: "Morning, evening, and noon will I call upon Thee." He had a method in prayer, and it is highly important that we should have. Many fail at this point. They are full of good intentions with regard to praying, but allow other things to crowd out the prayer hour. The day is full of interruptions. They live in a strain. People are continually going and coming, until they are too tired to pray. All cannot observe the same hour for praying, but all should have *some* hour, and then stick to it. To be sure, emergencies may arise when they cannot, but this is only an exception to the rule. "The morning watch" is the most favorable for communion with God. Moody said that he talked with God before he looked on the face of man. There are many things in favor of an early prayer hour. It prepares us for the duties of the day. It nerves us for conflict and strengthens us for trial.... *There must be time taken for prayer.* Nothing is more important, and we cannot afford to be cheated out of it. Shame on us, that we will even allow petty trivialities to break our engagement with the Most High....

Steps in the Prayer Life

[One writer] has suggested four steps in the prayer life: First, asking; second, asking in faith; third, asking in faith in the name of Jesus; and fourth, praying in the Holy Spirit. Anybody can ask—it is the first lesson, and it is the first condition of receiving. "Ask, and ye shall receive." For what should we ask? According to our needs. "In everything with prayer and supplications, and giving of thanks, let your requests be made known unto God." Prayer should cover every phase of life. It embraces all with which we have to do as well as the needs of this great, wide world. "According to your faith, so be it unto you" is the measure of receiving. How often we expect little and get little! "Whatsoever things ye desire when you pray, believe that you receive them, and ye shall have them"…. Just on the eve of His crucifixion, the Master said: "hitherto you have asked nothing in My name." "Ask and ye shall receive, that your joy may be full." Then the apostle exhorts, "Whatsoever you do in word or deed, let all be done in the name of the Lord Jesus." Few of us have any adequate conception of the power of that Name. "Wherefore God hath highly exalted Him and given Him a name that is above every name." "That at the name of Jesus every knee should bow, of things in heaven and things in earth, and things under the earth, and that every tongue should confess that Jesus Christ is Lord to the glory of God the Father." To pray in the name of Jesus doesn't mean to just get down and rattle off a few formal utterances or meaningless phrases, but it means that we shall be in such union with Christ that we will ask in harmony with His will and in humble reliance upon His merit. To pray thus is the same as if Jesus himself was making the request….

Praying in the Holy Spirit

So far in this treatise we have discussed prayer as follows: First, asking; second, asking in faith; and then praying in the name of Jesus. We now wish to speak particularly of a still more advanced stage in the prayer life. Perhaps it is not altogether correct to speak of it as an advanced stage, for this kind of praying is sometimes seen in the primary phases of Christian experience, and yet it more frequently operates in those who have gone deeper into the things of the Spirit. It is known under various appellations, such as inwrought prayer, prevailing prayer, and praying in the Holy Spirit. All true prayer is inwrought and through the Spirit, but not to such a marked degree, and this chapter is devoted to the consideration of this kind of praying—the times when the Holy Spirit travails through us until our own spirit is wrenched within us by a superhuman hand. This is not the ordinary prayer life. It is an operation of the Spirit somewhat out of the line of prayer generally pursued. However, while in the mighty throes of this travail the burden that comes upon you is a luxury, and may be accompanied by a thrill of rapture, or a spiritual uplift in some other form. While the soul is rent with the strong desire there may be the unutterable peace of God within. It is a time when the Spirit of God, who is always in His people, comes upon them mightily and pours out through them a torrent of infinite pleadings. These seasons are occasions of measureless value. They occur more often in some lives than others, but there are few, if any, among the devout who have not had some experiences of this kind. [There are] times when the whole prayer life [seems] to head up in some vast mountain peak of desire, and to vent itself in a Niagara of petition. Inexpressibly precious are hours like these, when the soul is so mightily stirred by the Spirit and expresses itself in an intensity of supplication as striking as it is unusual, and as far-reaching as the omnipotency of the Spirit.…

With regard to this kind of praying we would say: First, it doesn't come at our option—that is, we cannot offer a prayer of this kind unless God puts it on us. We may and should pray continuously and earnestly, but this particular kind of prayer can only be offered under pressure of the Spirit. We may go for weeks in a blessed prayer life without this wrench of soul. We may long for it and yet not have it. It comes unexpectedly. In some hard, drawn-out battles we pray on and on without this travail, and then suddenly it grips us and we are borne along its mighty current up to the very throne, "with strong crying," with supplication "and tears." It is not left for us to say when this heart-wrenching cry shall be given. God is a sovereign, and while we are to "pray without ceasing," He elects when such travail shall come upon us.

Neither is it left us to determine the subjects of such inwrought prayer. We would like to pray thus for so-and-so, but we may never do it. The heart doesn't break at our command. This inner wrench of spirit is not at our disposal. We are importuned to pray for this one and that one, and so we can in a general way, but the prayer in the Holy Spirit of which we are now speaking, comes at no man's bidding.

It may be for a member of your own family or it may be for some far-off missionary. It may be for a revival at some local church, or it may be for some interest remote; it matters not—it comes in unexpected ways and unexpected times. It may come upon you while walking on the street, on the farm or in the shop. Never neglect it. When thus pressed in spirit to pray do not disobey. Vital issues are involved. Such soul travail is profoundly significant....

Perhaps one reason why we cannot have such travail is because somebody else has travailed for them, and then there may be those who have so hardened themselves against the truth that prayer would be of no further avail, and we should not expect the Lord to put on us a spirit of prayer in such instances. We cannot pray in the same way for everybody. In a general sense prayer can be offered for all men, but this inwrought prevailing prayer we will not have for all men. It is given by the Spirit as the Lord pleaseth.

A word of caution is needed here lest we fix our attention on these extraordinary manifestations in the prayer life to the neglect of the ordinary and commonplace. The bulk of our praying will be along the usual lines of quiet waiting, thanksgiving and daily petition. We are not to wait for signs and wonders, but to go right along and pray. If we are inspired and controlled by the Spirit there will be an endless variety in our praying. Sometimes it will be a season of communion and fellowship with God. Then at other times the heart will be poured out in a torrent of intercession.

There was a timid knock heard at the study door. The minister opened it, and there stood a little boy. "What do you want, son," inquired the father. "Oh, papa. I just want to be with you awhile," was the reply, and so there are times when we just want to be closeted with God in ceaseless adoration. Then again, there are seasons when the Spirit within us cries out with longings that cannot be uttered. No two prayer experiences will be just alike. We are not to expect the wrench and twist in the heart all the time—it would be abnormal; but we are to walk in the Spirit and pray as He directs....

We can lay down no rule as to the tone and direction of the prayer, "for we know not what we should pray for as we ought," but the Holy Spirit will control in all these things if we lie passive in His hands. It is not for us to want to pray like somebody else, to be quiet or vehement in our devotions, but to live in God and let Him work in us and through us, according to His own good pleasure.

A further word of caution: Beware of praying only when you *feel* like it. Our feelings are very deceptive—they vary according to the physical condition. We have often gone to prayer when there was a heaviness of the flesh and suddenly found ourselves in a most delightful spirit of prayer, and then again the lethargic spirit would refuse to depart, but we just prayed on, anyway. We will not always be on the mountaintop even in our praying. We may be sorely oppressed by Satan while on our knees. The length of the prayer must be determined by your own illumined consciousness. You don't need to pray all day because somebody else does, neither do you need to cease praying in ten minutes because somebody else does. The prayer life of each individual should be formulated in harmony with the laws of his own being, and such will always be the case if the Spirit controls.

The Church stands greatly in need of good prayers, people who have given themselves wholly to the Lord, and whose every step is in the power of the Spirit. Such can be used wherever needed. What a privilege to so walk with God that we may be in momentary touch with every call of the Spirit! Surely every Christian should aspire to such a state. "The effectual, fervent prayer of the righteous man availeth much."

Correspondence with Dr. Phineas F. Bresee

The following correspondence with Dr. Phineas F. Bresee, founder of the Church of the Nazarene in the West, took place during 1907 and reflects McClurkan's interest in the Nazarenes but also his concerns about possible union with the Church of the Nazarene.

January 1, 1907

Dear Bro. Bresee:

Greetings in the name of the Lord. Things are moving along about as usual in the South. We have written for one of your Manuals, but haven't as yet received it. We have longed to see a movement of sufficient breadth and Spiritual force to embrace the Pentecostal people of the different temperaments and denominational bias. Our Mission is organized on this basis, but we need to form congregations if we follow up the work systematically, and we have been looking around for other kindred spirits with whom we might affiliate in such an organization. The Church of the Nazarene comes nearer our ideal than any other which we know, and yet there may be difficulties that would not be easily removed in the way of our union. The name is a very small matter, and so far as we are concerned, we are not particular about having any of our name in the united body, but it seems to us that yours is too long, could we not have a more simple appellation? As there is but one Church composed of all believers, might it not be well to recognize this fact in adopting some simple term, which would distinguish us from other bodies of Christians. Again our Missionary movement is quite an interest, we now have 28 Missionaries on the field, with others under appointment to go. How could this matter be adjusted? It has occurred to us that possibly our work has been peculiarly matters purely local, but when it comes to doctrinal statements and the general plan of work, we think that it had better be controlled by the entire body.

Third, as to doctrinal statement. The vast majority of our people are Arminian in their views, but we believe that we can accomplish the best results by working on a broader basis of doctrinal agreement than either of the two great ecclesiastical systems now extant. Neither [of] the extreme statements of [Calvinism] or Arminianism produce the best type of character. Our candid judgment is that the holiness movement as a body would be strengthened by a little more emphasis being put upon Grace. In our zeal to arouse a worldly church we have stressed works to such an extent that the Grace side has been neglected. We believe that there is more in the keeping power and faithfulness of God than many see.

We need less theory and more practice. The world cares but little for our shibboleths, but a symmetrical holy life will always command respect.

With regard to sanctification, we teach that we enter the sanctified life through consecration and faith, and then follows the perfecting of the character, the former an act, the latter a process. The sanctified life is synonymous with the Bible phrases "perfect heart" or "pure heart." We believe that there has not been enough teaching as to what follows sanctification, and as a result many sincere and devout people are confused as to the distinction between humanity and sin. If a holiness work is to become permanent one must avoid under-rating or over-rating these various processes of grace. It is not difficult to get people to profess beyond where they live and this will seriously cripple the work, for the community will judge us by the stern law of facts, hence the great need of careful discriminating teaching as to doctrine.

The above crude outline will give you an idea of the drift of our thought. What we desire is this: A statement narrow enough to include the essential features of entire consecration and cleansing, and broad enough to embrace all who believe we can have a pure and perfect heart and live a sanctified life.

We have organized only a few congregations in the Pentecostal Mission. We represent quite an interest and could set in order a goodly number of congregations in a short while were we so disposed. There has been so little unity of action as to organization among the Pentecostal people at large that we have held together chiefly as an inspiration and fellowship rather than by organization. But it seems to us now that we are at the parting of the way[s] and that we must either affiliate with the most spiritual organizations in the field among the older denominations, or we must make one of our own. Independence is exposed to too many dangers. Our hearts yearn for a fellowship with Pentecostal people on a broad scriptural basis stated as nearly as possible in Bible language. This would appeal to the devout of every temperament and school of thought. It does seem to us my dear brother that if kindred spirits all over the land would unite in hand and heart we could soon cover this country with centers of Pentecostal Evangelism that would be a mighty power for good.

We believe that holiness churches started during the past 28 years are too narrow to do this work, they lack in both depth of teaching and breadth of thought. We want something that embraces all the essential features of the holiness Church plus every advantage that comes to us from wider outlooks than some of these devout brethren had. We say this with all respect to these Holy men, but we have more light and must walk it.

Our Missionary work is prospering, we have about twenty-five missionaries now, with the prospect of some ten more within the next year. It would be a blessed thing to get this interest unified.

We like your spirit and we long for a larger fellowship with those engaged in a similar work with us, and in answer to your kind request that we write you frankly our convictions, we send this letter.

May the Lord graciously bless you in every way.

Ephesians 3:14-21.
Affectionately yours,
J. O. McClurkan

*NOTE: For the readability of the following letter, new paragraphs are indented and the word **and** has been substituted for the ampersand.*

August 1, 1907

Rev. J. O. McClurkan

My Dear Brother:

Your good letter came duly to hand. I am very glad to hear from you directly, as I have known your name for some time. What you say as to [the] necessity of things as to organization has been in our mind and heart from the beginning. A doctrinal basis of necessary belief should be very simple and embrace what is essential to holiness. All not essential to holiness should be relegated to personal liberty. We mean by "personal liberty" in belief, that a person has a right to hold it, and to recognize the same right in another to believe differently without fussing about it. We have [held] and do hold that any truth about which there can be two theories, and a person can be holy and believe either theory, may be safely, and should be, relegated to individual liberty, and is not sufficiently important to be our real message. We have acted upon the conviction that the great dispensational truth, that which makes us a dispensation is that Jesus Christ baptizes believers with the Holy Spirit, sanctifying and empowering them. Our unity is in the simplicity of necessary belief and the perfect liberty in reference to all other truth. All can agree on holiness without which no man shall see the Lord, and preach it and testify it, until nothing can keep up with it, and all can agree in it and agree that every one shall think for himself and not for others on things not essential to holiness. This I understand to be the gist of what you say and is the platform on which we stand and from which we work.

As to organization I ask[ed] the Pub[lishing] House to send you the Manual. We agreed if the Commissions of the two Churches agreed to some slight modifications to meet the notions of some extreme congregationalists who were in the Association of Pentecostal Churches and they have become the most enthusiastic of all. They felt that they needed for efficiency an organization sufficiently connected so there could be full combination and responsibility of all the parts. They sought this in union with us. We have prayerfully and carefully sought all the liberty possible for the individual Churches with a bond of [connection] strong enough to make us one, and thus multiply our possibilities. As to undenominational work, much no doubt can be done for a little, but it must pass away soon. Those who seek wide and lasting results must organize and by staying together build strongly for Him who has called us. I believe that the Lord is showing the Churches and the leaders this necessity. I am just in receipt of a letter from Rev. H. C. Morrison in which he says that there are many individual Church[es] in the South that should be in this union. Used as he is to preach for the Annual meeting of these churches in Texas he will be pleased with our approval to urge upon them the giving into the general union. I believe we are on the verge of a general union of all the holiness Churches who are <u>real</u>, and care more for the great truth than for some notion, or prejudice, or side issue, or interpretation.

This evidently must be the ground of union: In the great essential[s], unity; in non-essentials, liberty.

No one can tell how glad I would be for you and your people to come in, and for us all [three] to join hands, and by our united faith and multiplied power stretch out our hands to fill the earth with full salvation. I shall be glad to hear from you. With much love to all

I remain
Yours very truly
P. F. Bresee

Bibliography

Books

Bangs, Carl. *Arminius: A Study in the Dutch Reformation.* Nashville: Abingdon Press, 1971.

Barrus, Ben., Milton L. Baughn, and Thomas H. Campbell. *A People Called Cumberland Presbyterians.* Memphis: Frontier Press, 1972.

Benson, John T., Jr. *A History of the Pentecostal Mission, 1898–1915.* Nashville: Trevecca Press, 1977.

__________ . *Historic East Nashville and Old Tulip Street Methodist Church.* Nashville: Trevecca Press, 1980.

__________ . *Beginning Years, Tennessee District Pentecostal Church of the Nazarene, as per Minutes of 1912, 1913, 1914, and 1915.* Nashville: John T. Benson Publishing Co., 1976.

Bickerstaff, M. *There Was A Man Sent… An Outline of the Story of Howell Harris of Trevecka and the Calvinistic Methodist Church of Wales (now called the Presbyterian Church of Wales).* Trevecca: Stephens and George, 1959.

Chapman, J. B. *A History of the Church of the Nazarene.* Kansas City: Nazarene Publishing House, 1926.

Cook, J. E. *W. M. Tidwell (A Life That Counted): The Life of William Moses Tidwell.* Ann Arbor, Michigan: Malloy Lithographing, Inc., n.d.

Dayton, Donald W. *Theological Roots of Pentecostalism.* Grand Rapids: Francis Asbury Press, 1987.

Dieter, Melvin E. *The Holiness Revival of the Nineteenth Century.* Metuchen, N. J.: Scarecrow Press, 1980.

Evans, Eifion. *Howell Harris, Evangelist (1714-1773).* Cardiff: University of Wales Press, 1974.

Graham, Eleanor, ed. *Nashville: A Short History and Selected Buildings*. Nashville: Historical Commission of Metropolitan Nashville-Davidson County, 1974.

Harris, John. *G. Campbell Morgan: The Man and His Ministry*. New York: Fleming H. Revell Company, 1930.

Haynes, B. F. *Tempest-tossed on Methodist Seas*. Louisville: Pentecostal Publishing Company, 1921.

Heath, Merle McClurkan. *A Man Sent of God: The Life of J. O. McClurkan*. Kansas City: Beacon Hill Press, 1947.

Jones, Charles E. *Perfectionist Persuasion: The Holiness Movement and American Methodism, 1867–1936*. Metuchen, N.J.: Scarecrow Press, 1974.

__________. *A Guide to the Study of the Holiness Movement*. Metuchen, N.J.: Scarecrow Press, 1974.

Laird, Rebecca. *Ordained Women of the Church of the Nazarene*. Kansas City: Nazarene Publishing House, 1993.

McClurkan, J. O. *Wholly Sanctified: What It Is and How It May Be Obtained*. Nashville: Pentecostal Mission Publishing Company, n.d.

__________. *How to Keep Sanctified*. Nashville: Pentecostal Mission Publishing Company, 1903.

__________. *Behold He Cometh: A Series of Brief Lessons on the Second Coming of Christ*. Nashville: Pentecostal Book and Tract Depository, 1901.

__________. *Chosen Vessels*. Nashville: Pentecostal Mission Publishing Company, n.d.

__________. *Personal Work*. Nashville: Pentecostal Mission Publishing Company, 1914.

__________. *The Ministry of Prayer*. Nashville: Pentecostal Mission Publishing Company, n.d.

McDonald, B. W. *History of the Cumberland Presbyterian Church*. 4th ed. Nashville: Board of Publication of the Cumberland Presbyterian Church, 1899.

Mead, Frank S. *Handbook of Denominations in the United States*. 9th ed. Revised by Samuel S. Hill. Nashville: Abingdon Press, 1990.

Moments in History, 1898–1989. Nashville: First Church of the Nazarene, 1989.

Morgan, Jill. *A Man of the Word: Life of G. Campbell Morgan*. New York: F. H. Revell, 1951.

Nuttall, Geoffrey F. *Howell Harris, 1714–1773: The Last Enthusiast*. Cardiff: University of Wales Press, 1965.

Parker, J. Fred. *Into All the World: The Story of Nazarene Missions Through 1980*. Kansas City: Nazarene Publishing House, 1983.

Peters, John L. *Christian Perfection and American Methodism*. Nashville: Abingdon Press, 1956.

Pollock, John C. *The Keswick Story*. Chicago: Moody Press, 1964.

Purkiser, W. T. *Called unto Holiness.* Vol. 2, Kansas City: Nazarene Publishing House, 1983.

Redford, M. E. *The Rise of the Church of the Nazarene.* Kansas City: Beacon Hill Press, 1948.

Smith, Timothy L. *Called unto Holiness.* Kansas City: Nazarene Publishing House, 1962.

Strickland, S. W. *A New Look at Rev. J. O. McClurkan.* Nashville: The Parthenon Press, 1960.

Wynkoop, Mildred Bangs. *The Trevecca Story.* Nashville: Trevecca Press, 1976.

Articles

Darda, Nashville: Trevecca Nazarene College yearbook, 1928 and 1951.

Davies, Gareth. "Trevecka (1706–1964)," *Brycheiniog,* Vol. XV (1971), ed. D. J. Davies.

Dieter, Melvin. "The Development of Holiness Theology in Nineteenth Century America," *Wesleyan Theological Journal* 20, no. 1 (Spring 1985).

Hardy, C. E. Founder's Day Address at Trevecca Nazarene College. *Trevecca Messenger* (December 1946).

Herald of Holiness. Kansas City, Missouri: Church of the Nazarene, 31 October 1917, "Our Latest College." Also, 24 February 1915, "Union of the Pentecostal Mission and the Pentecostal Church of the Nazarene: Articles of Agreement."

Ingersol, Stan. "The New Testament Church of Christ: A Centennial Sketch," *Herald of Holiness* (June 1994).

Lane, Margaret. "The Queen of the Methodists," (The Countess of Huntingdon), *Brycheiniog,* Vol. XV (1971), ed. D. J. Davies.

Living Water. Nashville, Tennessee: Pentecostal Mission. 19 January 1905; 14 September 1905; 26 July 1906; 11 October 1906; 17 October 1907; 24 June 1909; 10 November 1910; 5 October 1911; 23 November 1911; 9 October 1913; 12 February 1914; 24 September 1914.

McClurkan, Emmett. Founder's Day Address at Trevecca Nazarene College. *Trevecca Messenger* (December 1945).

McClurkan, J. O. "Bible Training School," *Zion's Outlook,* 30 May 1901.

Myers, Lucia. "The Faith of Lady Huntingdon," *The New Christian Advocate* (December 1957).

Nashville American. "The Holiness Work in Lebanon," 14 August 1900.

Nashville Banner. "Beloved Man Passes Away," 16 September 1914.

Nashville Tennessean and the Nashville American. "Four Religious Conventions to Be Held this Week," 6 October 1911.

Nazarene Weekly. Paper of First Church of the Nazarene, Nashville, Tennesssee, 19 March 1972.

Raser, Harold E. "Holiness Movement" in *Dictionary of Christianity in America,* ed. Daniel G. Reid, 1990.

Redford, M. E. "Rev. J. O. McClurkan," *Herald of Holiness,* 16 July 1951.

Reynolds, H. F. "Union of the Pentecostal Mission with the Pentecostal Church of the Nazarene," *Other Sheep,* (March 1915).

Trevecca College for Christian Workers. 13th Annual Bulletin, 1913–1914.

Zion's Outlook. 22 September 1898; 28 February 1901; 7 March 1901; 11 April 1901; 30 May 1901; 15 August 1901; 22 August 1901; 7 November 1901; 28 November 1901.

Unpublished Material

Bresee, P. F. Letter to Rev. J. O. McClurkan, 1 August 1907.

Chilton, John. Interview with C. E. Hardy, S. W. Strickland, and Bobby Sulivan about J. O. McClurkan, November 1962. Trevecca Archives.

Cox, Edward. "Tennessee Nazarene History," Paper presented to the Tennessee District Church of the Nazarene Advisory Board, 29 January 1972.

Greathouse, William M. "Trevecca College: A Vine of God's Planting," Founder's Day Address at Trevecca Nazarene College, 14 November 1986.

Hiatt, R. Jeffrey. "A Study of the World Mission History of the Pentecostal Mission 1898–1915, and Its Contributions to the Development of the Mission, Polity, Personnel, Practices, Procedures and Growth of the Church of the Nazarene from 1907–1925," Unpublished Paper for the master of theology degree, Asbury Theological Seminary, August 1997.

Ingersol, Robert Stanley. "Burden of Dissent: Mary Lee Cagle and the Southern Holiness Movement," Ph.D. dissertation, Duke University, 1989.

McClurkan, J. O. Letter to P. F. Bresee, 1 January 1907.

"Minutes." Pentecostal Alliance and Pentecostal Mission, Nashville, Tennessee: 14 May 1898; 18-20 July 1898; 23-27 November 1899; 11 February 1901; 1 August 1901; 6 September 1901; 25 September 1901; 30 October—4 November 1901; 4 November 1901; 22 October 1904; 29 December 1904; 16 February 1905; 16 March 1905; 8 October 1905; 4-8 October 1906; 3-7 October 1907; 2 October 1908; 25 November 1908; 1 October 1909; 3 October 1910; 4 October 1910; 22 November 1910; 21 February 1911; 14 October 1911; 25 October 1912; 11 October 1914.

Nesbitt, William J. "The Primal Families of the Yellow Creek Valley," Unpublished document belonging to members of the Church of the Nazarene, Erin, Tennessee, 1985.

Pentecostal Mission Training Home for Girls. Nashville: Foster and Parres Company, 1913. Pamphlet in Trevecca Archives.

Redford, M. E. "History of the Church of the Nazarene in Tennessee," Unpublished B.D. thesis, Vanderbilt University, 1934.

Reed, Millard. "A Brief Study of the Pentecostal Mission," Unpublished Paper submitted to Professor Eugene Te Selle, Vanderbilt University, 20 December 1976.

Reynolds, H. F. Letter to E. P. Ellyson, 15 March 1911.

Taylor, Mendell. "Historical Documents of the Church of the Nazarene," Unpublished Collection of Documents at Nazarene Theological Seminary, n.d.

Wall, Howard, Jr. Founder's Day Address at Trevecca Nazarene College, 11 November 1966.

White, Jasper. "A Man and a Mission: The Story of J. O. McClurkan and the Pentecostal Mission," Unpublished master's thesis, Indiana Central College, May 1973.

Williams, Eugene. "History of Trevecca Nazarene College," Unpublished B.D. thesis, Nazarene Theological Seminary, 1956.

Appendix

Historical Calendar

1768   August 24. Trevecka College opened in Trevecka, Wales

1779   James Robertson established first permanent settlement in Nashville

1796   Tennessee became the sixteenth state in the Union

1800   The "Great Revival" in Kentucky and Tennessee—Out of this revival came the Cumberland Presbyterian Church, organized in 1810 at Montgomery Bell State Park in Dickson County, Tennessee

1843   Wesleyan Methodist Church, a Wesleyan-holiness denomination, organized

1860   Free Methodist Church, a Wesleyan-holiness denomination, organized

1861   Civil War began—Tennessee the last state to secede from the Union

1861   November 13. James Octavias McClurkan born in Houston County, Tennessee, between Dickson and Erin, in Yellow Creek Community

1866   Tennessee became the first Confederate state to re-enter the Union

1867   National Association for the Promotion of Holiness organized in Vineland, New Jersey

1868   Bible Prophetic Conference organized in Niagara, New York

1875   McClurkan converted in revival at the old Bethany Cumberland Presbyterian Church in Yellow Creek, Houston County, Tennessee

1875   Keswick Higher Life Movement began in England, inspired by the labors of American holiness evangelists on English soil

1879   McClurkan licensed to preach by the Charlotte Presbytery of the Tennessee Cumberland Presbyterian Church

1880   Salvation Army, a Wesleyan-holiness religious group founded in London, England, by William Booth in 1875, came to America

1881   Beginnings of what came to be called the Christian and Missionary Alliance, founded by A. B. Simpson, a Keswick-holiness "denomination"

1881   Church of God (Anderson, Indiana), a Wesleyan-holiness denomination, begun— founded by Daniel S. Warner

1882   November 15. McClurkan married Martha Frances Rye

1886   McClurkan began his pastoral ministry in the Cumberland Presbyterian Church in Decatur, Texas

1887   July 21. Organization of the People's Evangelical Church, the oldest independent congregation later to become a part of the Church of the Nazarene, in Rhode Island under the leadership of Rev. Fred Hillery

1888   McClurkan went to California to pastor

1888   Cyrus I. Scofield popularized premillennial dispensationalism in his *Rightly Dividing the Word of Truth* and in the Scofield Bible (1909)

1890   Asbury College founded as a Wesleyan-holiness institution in Wilmore, Kentucky

1893   June. Robert Lee Harris, former Methodist holiness evangelist, held revivals in West Tennessee including one at Milan, Tennessee, at the invitation of Mrs. Donie Mitchum, a sanctified Methodist Sunday school teacher

1894   July 5. Organization of the New Testament Church of Christ under former Methodist holiness evangelist, Robert Lee Harris, in Milan, Tennessee— This church was the first Nazarene root in the South. The New Testament Church of Christ merged with C. B. Jernigan's Independent Holiness Church in Texas in 1905 to form the Holiness Church of Christ, which then united with the Pentecostal Church of the Nazarene in 1908 at Pilot Point, Texas.

1894   Holiness movement entered Middle Tennessee, according to B. F. Haynes, and revival swept through Erin, Charlotte, Dickson, Clarksville, Franklin, and Nashville—It appears that a "holiness house church" may have developed out of the revival in Erin, Tennessee, sometime between 1894 and 1896. The Erin congregation may be the *oldest church in the South in continuous existence* that became a part of the Church of the Nazarene.

1895   McClurkan sanctified under the ministry of the Methodist holiness evangelist, Beverly Carradine, in San Jose, California, and began his holiness ministry

1895   October 20. Church of the Nazarene begun in Los Angeles, California, under the leadership of Phineas F. Bresee

1897   McClurkan arrived back in Tennessee in the early months and preached in a revival led by his boyhood friend and brother-in-law, Jim Rye, who became the first fruits of McClurkan's holiness preaching in Middle Tennessee

1897   McClurkan's only son became ill in the summer—Emmet McClurkan's illness required the family to come to Nashville for medical care. McClurkan conducted revival meetings in Nashville during his son's extended illness. John T. and Eva Benson and others were sanctified under McClurkan's holiness preaching.

1897   McClurkan held services for his holiness flock in Nashville during the winter months of 1897-1898 in the Conservatory of Music building on the corner of Fifth Avenue and Cedar Street. These services mark the early beginnings of Nashville's First Church of the Nazarene.

1898   May 14. First organizational move toward forming a fellowship of holiness people in Middle Tennessee—Obtained use of old Tulip Street Methodist Church

1898   June 8. McClurkan became superintendent of holiness work in Nashville and Middle Tennessee— July. Organization created called the Pentecostal Alliance

1899   Name of National Association for the Promotion of Holiness changed to National Holiness Association (name changed again in 1970 to Christian Holiness Association and in 1997 to Christian Holiness Partnership)

1899   Texas Holiness University founded at Peniel, Texas, with A. M. Hills as the first president—It is the oldest Nazarene college and is known today as Southern Nazarene University.

1900   McClurkan's group took over the religious paper, the *Zion's Outlook*, from B. F. Haynes

1900   November. Pentecostal Alliance moved to old Hynes School building at Fifth and Jo Johnston north of the State Capitol

1900–1901 Pastor's Class began in McClurkan's study in winter months—birth of "Trevecca"

1901   Pentecostal Alliance name changed to Pentecostal Mission

1901   November 5. The Pentecostal Literary and Bible Training School opened in the old Hynes School building

1901   Organization of the Independent Holiness Church at Van Alstyne, Texas, under the leadership of Rev. C. B. Jernigan—This group merged with the New Testament Church of Christ in 1905 to form the Holiness Church of Christ, which then united with the Pentecostal Church of the Nazarene in 1908 at Pilot Point, Texas.

1902   Pentecostal Mission incorporated under the state laws of Tennessee— Pentecostal Mission Publishing Company founded

1902   Pentecostal Mission's Training Home for Girls (orphanage) begun under the leadership of Mrs. Tim H. Moore

1903   Name of *Zion's Outlook* weekly paper changed to *Living Water*, still edited by J. O. McClurkan

1905   Pentecostal Mission and Bible School moved to 125 Fourth Avenue North behind the Ryman Auditorium

1907   Correspondence between McClurkan and Bresee about church union—McClurkan's group invited to send representatives to attend the October 1907 Chicago Assembly which united East and West under the name of Pentecostal Church of the Nazarene

1907   June. Pentecostal Mission's Door of Hope Rescue Home for unfortunate girls begun under the leadership of Mrs. Burges

1908   McClurkan and Pentecostal Mission representatives attended the General Assembly of the Pentecostal Church of the Nazarene at Pilot Point, Texas, at which time the Holiness Church of Christ in the Southwest joined with the Nazarenes, a union which is considered the official birth of the Nazarene denomination

1910   October. The Nazarene delegation of Bresee, Reynolds, Ellyson, and Robinson met in Nashville with McClurkan's group to discuss church union—No agreement reached on union

1910   November. School name changed to "Trevecca College for Christian Workers," a change which included becoming a "four-year college"—Name "Trevecca" taken from a school in Wales started by Lady Huntingdon in 1768 and means "a binding together in love"

1910   Trevecca Hospital established at 125 Eighth Avenue South with C. E. Hardy as superintendent

1911   October. The 3rd General Assembly of the Pentecostal Church of the Nazarene met in Nashville—E. F. Walker elected general superintendent and B. F. Haynes elected as the first editor of the *Herald of Holiness*

1914   McClurkan negotiated for the Percy Warner estate on Gallatin Road and made preparations to move Trevecca to it by September

1914   September 16. J. O. McClurkan died of typhoid fever at age 52

1914   December. C. E. Hardy succeeded McClurkan as pastor of the Pentecostal Tabernacle (later First Church of the Nazarene) in Nashville, Tennessee

1915   February 13. Articles of Agreement signed for Pentecostal Mission to unite with the Pentecostal Church of the Nazarene

1915   July. C. E. Hardy elected president of Trevecca College

1917   September. Trevecca College officially adopted by the Pentecostal Church of the Nazarene

1917   First Church of the Nazarene moved across the river to 510 Woodland Street after purchasing and remodeling the old Presbyterian Church severely damaged by the great East Nashville fire of 1916

Pastors of Pentecostal Tabernacle/First Church of the Nazarene, Nashville, Tennessee

J. O. McClurkan	1897–1914
C. E. Hardy	1914–1916
R. T. Williams	1916–1918
G. E. Waddle	1918–1919
E. A. Girvin	1920–1921
H. H. Wise	1921–1948
E. K. Hardy	1948–1952
C. D. Ewell	1952–1957
W. M. Greathouse	1958–1963
T. E. Martin	1963–1970
J. V. Morsch	1970–1974
Millard C. Reed	1974–1991
Stanley A. Toler	1991–1994
Gary A. Henecke	1994–Present

Presidents of Trevecca Nazarene University

J. O. McClurkan	1901–1914
C. E. Hardy	1915–1919
S. S. White	1919–1920
C. E. Hardy	1920–1925
John T. Benson	1925–1926
A. O. Hendricks	1926–1928
C. E. Hardy	1928–1936
A. B. Mackey	1936–1963
W. M. Greathouse	1963–1968
Mark R. Moore	1968–1979
Homer J. Adams	1979–1991
Millard C. Reed	1991–PRESENT

Index

An italicized number refers to a photograph on that page